OR 6.1.94

The Thames:
Record of a Working Waterway

The Thames:
Record of a Working Waterway

David Gordon Wilson

B. T. Batsford Ltd · London

Acknowledgements

I am grateful for the helpful information and material received over a number of years from: Dr Mary Prior, Tony Ellis, John Gould, Malcolm Graham, Mike Hall, Peter Marsden, Sean McGrail, Dr Martin de Weerd; and my colleagues, lock keepers Lyn David, Alan Hastings, Bill McCreadie, Brian Rogers and Brian Webb, not forgetting the rivermen, tug skippers and bargemen of the Thames.

I thank Dorothy Hague for her beautiful calligraphy on the map and my wife, Roma, for translating my scribble into a readable typescript.

Extracts from the published Buckinghamshire Quarter Sessions Records appear by permission of the Bucks County Record Office, and translations of Crown Copyright Records in the Public Record Office by permission of the Controller of H.M. Stationery Office.

Some illustration captions include the names of the artists whose works can be found in the bibliography. Other illustrations not credited in the caption or listed below are from my own collection.

I give my thanks to the individuals and organizations for their permission to reproduce the following illustrations: J. Brooks and H. Horsham, 71, 96; G. Collier, 64; L. David, 37; G. Fielder, 70; J. French, 2; E. M. Hazleton, 9, 48; N. Leaver, 82; Miss E. A. Upson, 56; M. E. Ware, 81, 100; Dr M. D. de Weerd, 22; Aylesbury Museum, 39; The National Trust, 28; Oxfordshire County Libraries, 26, 60, 66, 67, 73, 76, 99; The Tate Gallery, London, 31; Thames Water, Reading, 4, 6, 12, 13, 46, 49, 74, 75, 77, 78, 80, 86, 87, 88, 89, 90; by courtesy of the Trustees of the Victoria and Albert Museum, 92, 93.

© David Gordon Wilson 1987
First published 1987

ISBN 0 7134 5298 6

Typeset by Latimer Trend & Company Ltd, Plymouth
and printed by Anchor Brendon Ltd, Tiptree, Essex

for the publishers
B. T. Batsford Ltd
4 Fitzhardinge Street
London
W1H 0AH

Contents

Introduction

The Thames probably has a longer history of human use and physical alteration than any other river in Britain. For thousands of years people have hunted and farmed its banks, fished in its waters and ground corn with its power. People have also poled, rowed, paddled and sailed along its course, not only for pleasure (that is a comparatively recent phenomenon) but as traders, bringing vital supplies into the English countryside and taking heavy cargoes back with the stream to London River.

Much is already known about the development of the river for navigation, but the history of the commercial craft for which it was developed has always been a neglected subject. The trading craft of the freshwater Thames were known as Western or West Country barges. They have intrigued me ever since reading Fred Thacker's *Thames Highway*, but I have found that very few writers, including Thacker, have attempted to describe them or explain how they were operated. When in 1970 I approached the National Maritime Museum and other establishments for information, all I received was a list of books on tideway spritsail barges, and an article on how to build a Thames punt.

Even a painstaking researcher such as the late Eric McKee in his *Working Boats of Britain*, which is introduced as the most comprehensive single study of the working craft of a country, stated that he did not cover canal and river barges, as they have been so well described elsewhere. To illustrate how unfamiliar Western barges are, even to inland waterway historians, Michael Ware includes a copy of a painting of the River Itchen at Blackbridge, Winchester in his excellent *Britain's Lost Waterways* – and describes it as a 'fanciful view' because it depicts a large punt-like barge, laden with bales and barrels, and with a canvas awning over the aft end. In fact it is a typical Western barge, showing that the form was not entirely restricted to the Thames. It is astonishing

that craft which for hundreds of years supplied the Capital with so many essential products from the heart of England have been ignored for so long.

In 1977 my previous work with a local history society, combined with long-standing Thames interests, culminated in the publication of *The Making of the Middle Thames*, which partly dealt with the history of commerce on the river. Hundreds of other Thames books have been published, many of them extensively copied from earlier and often better works. In this version of the development of navigation I have tried to avoid using the standard examples of legislation so well recorded by Thacker and others, but some duplication is hard to avoid. If I am guilty of it I have tried to give acknowledgement to the writer concerned, hoping that others will do the same for me in the future.

The chapters on the history of the freshwater Thames are in chronological order, apart from some deviations to describe the connecting canals and the development of barges of a particular period. The history of the Port of London and the craft of the tidal river is treated as a separate and final chapter, for the Thames becomes a totally different entity below Teddington.

The bargemen of the Thames were, and still are, experts requiring skills and knowledge foreign to sailors of the unencumbered open waters. Generations lived in a secret linear world hardly suspected by the writers of their day. In their everyday, sometimes hazardous, working lives they performed a vital service, which has so often been ignored or depreciated in favour of glossy descriptions of riverside abbeys, mansions and picturesque scenery. I have tried to reveal just a little of their world, and hope that others committed to deeper academic research will be encouraged to uncover much more of the real history of the River Thames.

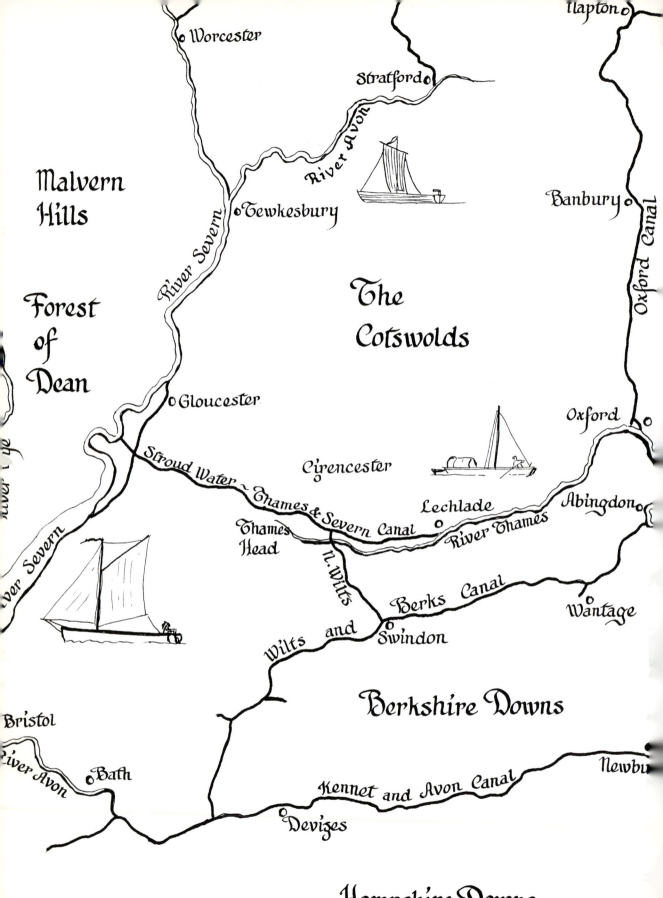

The River Thames

and connecting navigations

circa 1830

Northampton

Grand

Aylesbury

Junction

Chiltern Hills

Canal

Hertford

River Stort

River Lee

R. Roding

Wallingford

Marlow

Hedsor

Henley

Maidenhead

Paddington Arm

Regents Canal

Brentford

Gravese

London

Windsor

Richmond

Teddington

Weybridge

r Kennet

ding

singstoke

Basingstoke Canal

River Wey

Guildford

1 Early navigation

THE PREHISTORIC RIVER

Many of those who think they know the Thames – but do not live beside or work upon it – see only its placid, apparently tamed face in summer – not appreciating that it is an ever-changing living force, fed by innumerable arteries and draining about 5000 square miles of Southern England. Winter rains annually recharge the water table in the Cotswold limestones, the chalk of the Chilterns and Berkshire Downs, and even during a rainless summer there can still be a good flow of water in the main river from countless springs and tributaries. Winter spates annually scour the bed and bring down thousands of tons of silts, gravels and other debris which build up shoals before being eventually swept out to sea. But all rivers find the lowest and easiest course and a new channel will eventually be cut around any obstruction. Therefore – although perhaps not particularly reliable during drought or flood or when man asked too much of it, being in the main a slow running lowland river of good capacity – from early times the Thames provided a channel for navigation into the heart of England. Through the centuries generations of tough and resourceful navigators, the fishermen, fowlers, reed and rush cutters, and particularly the trading bargemen, moved along its course. They were an independent breed, close but not tied to the land, with an intimate knowledge of the river and its ways. With an expertise now long forgotten they towed, sailed, rowed and shoved their craft wherever there was water to float them.

Although there is no direct evidence of skin or hide-covered boats ever being used in the Thames basin, either coracles or the larger curraghs, there can be little doubt that from about 10,000 years ago some form of water transport was being poled or paddled on the main river and side streams, which compared to the earlier barrenness and great inundations at the end of the Ice Age, were now flowing placidly through a well-favoured afforested landscape.

In recent times the use of coracles, primarily for fishing, was restricted to Wales, the Severn region and Scotland. But in the Mesolithic, or Middle Stone Age period, before the introduction of metal tools to fashion more substantial craft, it is highly likely that the hunter/gatherer tribes – that left so many signs of their camp sites, in the form of thousands of stone implements on the banks of tributaries such as the Loddon and Kennet – used skin boats in a similar fashion to the salmon fishermen of West Wales today.

Larger sea-going craft, with keels and ribs covered with hide, similar to modern Irish curraghs, are mentioned by Caesar, being used in Southern Britain in 55 BC. Later Roman writers, notably Pliny in the first century AD, also mention them in connection with the transportation of tin and lead from Cornwall to the Isle of Wight port of transhipment to Gaul. Thus we may surmise that similar trading craft were also well-known on the Thames.

Because of their ease of construction and the abundance of willow, the tree whose branches supplied so many constructional needs for communities through the ages, skin and wickerwork boats predominated in the Stone Age.

In many parts of the world people using stone tools could, and still do, fashion dugouts from

1   A typical upper Thames winter spate. The deep meandering channel has practically disappeared, as run-off from the Cotswolds fills it to capacity and the river escapes across its flood plain

softwood trees. However, dugout boats, or to use the recently adopted term, logboats, do not appear to have been made here in the Stone Age. The many that have been recovered from riverbeds and peat-bogs all over lowland Britain are invariably made from large forest oak trees, either from a whole trunk or split half. Oak being a very hard wood is thought to have been impossible to work with stone tools, even with the help of fire, and therefore these boats cannot be older than the introduction of suitable metal tools in the Middle Bronze Age.

Very few of the British boats have been dated scientifically, using radio-carbon analysis. Those that have produce an amazing range of dates, from the Bronze Age right up to the Middle Ages. The use of logboats is well documented in Wales up to the sixteenth century, Ireland in the seventeenth, and Scotland and England in the eighteenth. At least one

seventeenth-century painting, of the Thames at Windsor, depicts craft which look very much like logboats.

Sean McGrain, in his classic study *Logboats of England and Wales*, lists 25 craft, in various states of fragmentation, recovered from the lower Thames basin, including the rivers Lee and Wey. None have so far been radio-carbon dated, neither is it yet possible to date them by construction details or size. As with all British examples, shapes vary widely, from some rounded canoe forms, such as the most recently found 18ft (5.7m) boat from Walton, to flat-bottomed, square-ended craft, shaped like relatively modern fishing and rush gathering punts, and capable of performing the same functions.

Of this latter type, one found in 1911 at Kew during dredging operations was about 14ft (4.5m) in length and 2ft 6in (0.75m) in beam, cut very square and with a central bulkhead, making two compartments. A similar but larger flat-bottomed boat was dredged from much higher up the Thames in 1872, near what was then known as Marlow Road Station

and now Bourne End, Bucks. This was 25ft (7.6m) in length and 3ft 3in (1m) in beam. Three broad transverse ridges were across the floor. The stern was square, but the bow was said to be pointed, with an upward curve.[1]

The Thames estuary extended an open invitation to the seafarers and traders of the Bronze Age who left a scattering of tools and weapons along practically the entire length of the river bed. Many bronze spearheads, daggers and swords dredged particularly from the middle Thames may have been thrown in as offerings to the river god. Others sank without trace when trading vessels were wrecked – perhaps in floodwater – whilst trying to work their way upstream, and still more lost during pitched battles between rival tribes fighting from war canoes.

None of the more sophisticated types of plank-built boats which are known to have been used in England in the Bronze Age have so far been discovered on the Thames. Our earliest examples, discovered in the bed of the tidal river, are the so-called Celtic craft of the Romano-British period, to be

2 Godstow weir pool, looking downstream towards Oxford, c. 1890. The original navigation channel before a new lock-cut bypassed it in 1790. The central shoal below the weir was a feature of many flash locks. To complement the text the reader must imagine the students are Iron Age tribesmen in a dugout canoe

discussed in the chapter on the evolution of the Western barges.

Discoveries from the air of cropmarks of large groups of burial mounds on the banks of the stripling Thames above Lechlade, wooden piles of a later Bronze Age wharf or island trading settlement excavated at Runnymede Bridge, and another possible very similar site near Wallingford, are just some examples of many showing that throughout its length, from at least the Bronze Age, water levels have not been significantly different from what they are today. Apart from some post-glacial braiding, the river has always sought the easiest course within one main channel, its meanders cutting and drifting across the flood plain. During the Bronze Age, because the countryside was still partly covered in forest, there was not the flash-flooding and great deposition of fine silts across the flood plain which, according to evidence from excavations in the Oxford area, only began to occur as the countryside was extensively ploughed from the Iron Age onwards.

Cropmarks show that most gravel terraces above winter flood levels were settled and farmed in prehistoric times, and later Saxon towns and villages occupy similar riverside sites, but apart from Bronze and Iron Age finds, possibly including some of the undated logboats dredged from the river bed, hard evidence for prehistoric non-tidal Thames navigation is scanty. One can only reason, for instance, that the absence of east/west roads in the middle Thames valley during the Romano-British period indicates that the river may have been used by barge traffic between Londinium and large grain producing estates, such as at Hambleden, near Henley.

The Romans made extensive use of inland waterways for trade and communications on the continent, and therefore it is inconceivable that they did not do likewise during their long occupation of Britain. Special auxiliary companies of native boatmen, recruited from the Rhineland, may well have brought their craft with them in the early years, but the flat-bottomed Celtic barges may have already been here, brought over by earlier invaders from Gaul.

As British trade developed, river crossings such as at Staines and Oxford may have become important for the transfer of heavy goods from barges to carts for distribution inland. At the Roman town of Dorchester (Oxfordshire) barges could have moved up the River Thame tributary to tie up almost beneath the town walls. The second-century A.D. Celtic barge excavated at Blackfriars in 1962 and found to have been carrying Kentish ragstone from the Medway, may well have had sister-ships carrying building materials, such as timber, bricks and tiles, from the Thames Valley to discharge them at a wharf close to where their successors were tying up a thousand years later.

MAN-MADE OBSTRUCTIONS

The Saxon settlers who colonized the valley during the Dark Ages established many of the Thames-side towns and villages which we know today. They

came in graceful craft which were clinker-built, with overlapping strakes, or planks, and left a legacy to the Thames of similarly constructed small rowing craft, such as wherries, peter boats, dinghies and skiffs. They also harnessed the power of rivers and streams for corn grinding, and by the Domesday Survey of 1086 Thames mills and probably their attendant mill dams were established at most of the villages and towns from Oxford to Bray, where modern locks and weirs exist today. There are eleventh-century references to river communication between Oxford, Abingdon, Wallingford and Reading, and therefore it is possible that flash locks – the means by which large craft passed through the mill dams – were already in use.

In 1197 Richard I ordered that all weirs on the Thames were to be removed, and in the same year 'quit-claimed all that which the Keeper of our Tower of London was wont yearly to have received of the said weirs ... that great detrement and inconvenience hath grown to our said City of London and also to the whole realm, by occasion of the said weirs.' However, this Act, and the many which followed, was probably aimed at unauthorized fish weirs, which lay partly across the channel and in backwaters. The term 'weir' may have originally meant a fish-trap but was gradually corrupted to include the mill dams in which fish-traps were usually incorporated.

Richard also obtained desperately-needed money by selling his inherent rights to the Thames to the City of London, although the river still remained 'the King's Highway'. The Corporation was able to exercise a certain influence up as far as Staines for centuries to follow, but it had very little control above there. Barges were soon proceeding all the way from London to Oxford, which by the early fourteenth century was to grow into one of the wealthiest provincial towns in England. In 1205 King John granted letters patent to 'William son of Andrew our servant that he might have while he lived one ship going and returning upon the Thames between Oxford and London with his property and merchandise free and unmolested by any toll and exaction which belongs to us; and that he might freely and without hindrance load that vessel wherever on the Thames he desired between Oxford and London.'[2]

In 1234 Henry II supplied a hundred oaks from

3 Streatley Mill, *c.* 1880. A typical Thames corn mill site dating from medieval times

4 'New Lock' Hurley, *c.* 1860. One of many ancient mill dams which survived until the late nineteenth century construction of flood relief weirs by the Thames Conservancy. The flash lock was on the far right, with the last remaining capstan standing to the right of the boat house

Savernake forest to help in the building of the Hospital of St John at Oxford, the timber being sent from Reading by water.[3] Throughout the century thousands of tons of building materials, mainly stone, were transported along the river for the building of castles and abbeys. For instance, in 1245 the Abbot of Medmenham was allowed to carry stone from the new works at Windsor Castle for the building of the Abbey. Medieval road transport was very primitive; therefore river navigation became essential, and many acts to improve the Thames for barge traffic throughout the following centuries illustrate the long and bitter conflict between the economically important but localized milling and fishing interests, and the nationally important trading links between the City of London and inland towns. There are also early allusions to river improvement by dredging and removal of shoals, such as in 1274 when the King decreed that 'the water of Thames (was) to be widened that ships and great

barges might ascend from London to Oxford, and descend . . . without hindrance from any weirs . . . as the Thames was so narrowed in divers places.'

The river above Oxford was, and still is, totally different in character to below, much narrower and more tortuous but retaining a good head of water flowing out of the Cotswold limestone water table. Place names such as Kempsford, Duxford, Shifford and Swinford show that here and there the river could once be crossed on foot, and some of the fords are extremely ancient. Recent discoveries at Kempsford, above Lechlade, appear to prove that this crossing was used in prehistoric times. A Roman track lines up with it, it was the site of a battle in AD 802 and it continued in use until the modern era. However, the number of fish weirs which later developed between Lechlade and Oxford may have heightened river levels enough to make fording impracticable, for by 1269 the ford at Shifford had been replaced by a lucrative ferry owned by the Abbot of Eynsham – and it was still in use in 1426.

Apart from an increase in road traffic, it may have been the increased depth of the upper river in the

5   The Hurley capstan, 1972, with a local resident to show its scale

thirteenth century which required that stone bridges were built at Lechlade, Radcot, Newbridge and Godstow. They have proved their worth as economic and strategic river crossings throughout the centuries but have adversely affected the river. Apart from accentuating flooding by restriction of water flow, the narrow medieval arches also restricted the size of barges working above Oxford. Old Godstow Bridge, the first going west from Oxford, today has a maximum width of 12ft (3.66m). When rebuilt, at the end of the nineteenth century, the builders probably utilized the original piers, for the maximum beam of barges trading to Lechlade, before the bridge was by-passed by the pound-lock in 1790, was stated as 11ft 9in (3.58m). Therefore the width of this bridge probably dictated the width of the Thames and Severn Canal locks, which took Thames barges.

Radcot Bridge, on the road between Faringdon and Bampton, has long been famous for its wharf from which, in the seventeenth century, were shipped large quantities of stone from the Taynton Quarries, near Burford, for Sir Christopher Wren's rebuilding of St Paul's Cathedral. Radcot was in a favourable position to cater for trade between Oxford and the (at that time) important up-river towns of Faringdon and Bampton, but early records are few. In 1271 a local yeoman was granted the craft of drowned boatman Gilbert, son of Walter Le Messer, and its contents, which included five-and-a-half quarters of wheat. In 1279 a cartulary of Beaulieu Abbey (which held Faringdon) reveals that the barges of grain merchants were using Radcot Wharf.[4] Radcot had also been granted a fair and market, so other goods were almost certainly traded along the upper river. Taynton stone came down river in 1293 for the building of St Stephen's Chapel, Westminster, although obstructions up river may have made it necessary to ship it from Abingdon.[5]

Ever since the Thames-side villagers established their cornmills and attendant dams, many uses were found for the power which the wheels generated and

6 Ridges Weir, below Newbridge, 1865. One of a number demolished in the early years of the Thames Conservancy. The right-hand side is a paddle and rymer flash lock. Hoop nets hang drying, ready to be lowered into the weir in place of the sluice gates

mills became an important part of the economic life of the valley. No history of Thames navigation would be complete without trying to explain how the navigators passed the dams which grew as the mills grew, and how they coped with the exactions inflicted by the millers, who naturally were sometimes loath to lose a good head of water by opening the dam for the passage of barges.

FLASH LOCKS

Although Darius cut a canal from the Nile to the Red Sea in 510 BC, and the Romans dug a few here and there in Europe, the first known example of simple gates being used to hold back water, and also allow boats to pass from one level to the next, was as early as about AD 70, on a canal in China. Here the

method used was merely to slide timbers in and out of vertical slots cut into abutment walls, a method which is still used to retain water in British canals when a serious leak occurs in an embankment. Other systems used in China included double slipways and vertical (or portcullis) gates. The 600 mile (1000 k) Grand Canal, which was completed in A.D. 610, in the tenth century apparently had vertical gates fitted only metres apart, in effect making the first pound locks. It is not until the thirteenth century that vertical or so-called portcullis gates and beam-and-paddle weirs came into use on canals in Flanders, Italy and Germany. In Holland, the tidal flood sluices had vertical gates for navigation, and these were later used in similar situations in eastern England, where they are known as staunches.[6] The beam-and-paddle weirs, which were found to be more suitable for use on the Thames, were known as flash locks. These are not to be confused with the pound locks which came later. The term *lock* seems to have originally meant a narrow passageway for barges, for some bridge

7 Mending hoop nets, 1875. The child fishes from a standard Thames punt, which has a well under the thwart for holding fish

arches were also called locks, particularly at London Bridge.

The early Thames mill dams were timber and rubble structures which stretched the full width of the main stream and were maintained and repaired by the miller, sometimes with special grants of timber from the Lord of the Manor. As is the case with modern overfall or lasher weirs, mill dams increased natural river levels by holding water back during periods of low rates of flow and as levels rose after rain automatically allowed excess water to overspill and pass down from dam to dam in a series of shallow steps to the sea. Usually there were also sluice gates built into the dam which could be drawn to alleviate flooding. The weirs which evolved from

them have been greatly increased in height over the centuries, but large modern gates now allow a fairly unimpeded flow to the sea when the river is in spate. The capacity of the channel then dictates whether there is to be flooding or not.

The early trading barges may have had to be dragged around the mill dams on rollers after the cargo had been unloaded, or winched through narrow by-pass channels, such as existed alongside fish weirs on the upper Severn into the nineteenth century. But soon bigger barges, perhaps carrying tons of stone from the Oxfordshire quarries and captained by a breed of resourceful river men, may have found it quite easy just to keep on going when they reached some charming rustic construction and simply force a way through the sagging timbers. Millers probably found that it was much cheaper in the long run to supply an opening in their dams so that barges could pass through in a slightly more orderly fashion. Passages were provided in the sec-

8   Drawing the tackle of a flash lock, 1875. In fact the engraving is incorrect. The keeper is shown trying to pull out a paddle which could not have been placed there without the support of an outside rymer. (H. R. Robertson)

tion of dam which may already have had 'paddle and rymer' tackle, which was taken out or closed in to control water levels.

A few paddle weirs are still used on the Thames today. Basically they consist of a slightly raised cill fixed across the bed of the river with slots just over 4in (10cm) wide on the upstream side about 2ft (60cm) apart. There is a corresponding slotted wooden beam and walkway directly above. Four-inch (10cm) square wooden rymer posts are held by the weir keeper (the lock-keeper) on the walkway and 'pitched' at an angle upstream against the current; with judgement, and sometimes luck, these eventually rest in the top and bottom slots. Wooden boards, about 2ft wide by 3ft deep (60cm × 100cm), on the end of long poles, are then thrust down to the bottom cill and the weight of water holds them against the rymers. The paddles can be two or three deep, depending on the 'head' of water to be maintained. The operation of a paddle and rymer weir is hazardous and requires skill and strength, particularly in the dark during spates when a twisted mass of weeds and branches may have been swept down to jam against the posts.

All that was originally required to make the structure into a flash lock was that, after the removal of the paddles and rymer posts, the rymer beam was taken out and the catwalk, which was counterbalanced like pound lock gates, could be swung back on a pivot-post set into the bank or dam. The width of the opening to take the largest barges in the eighteenth century was about 20ft (6m); in other words about ten sets of paddles.

On the downward passage a barge, or more likely several vessels, would send a crew member miles ahead to arrange with the miller for the flash lock to be opened. This had to be done at the right time, otherwise the levels in the reach might drop too soon and make the vessels go aground before they reached the lock. After the lock tackle had been drawn the levels would gradually fall above the lock and rise below. The length of time taken for the levels to nearly equalize depended on the height of the dam and the length of the reach between mills, which varied from less than a mile to over six. An impression of a barge passing through, based upon the account of pleasure boaters in small rowing boats occasionally using the remaining flash locks west of Oxford in Victorian times, might be as follows:

nearing the opening the craft would pick up momentum, the tillermen straining against the pull of the huge wooden rudder, other crew members endeavouring to keep a straight course with long sweeps or poles. Then with a rush they were through into the white water, where they would pray that the 'flash' or flush of water was strong enough to carry them across the shallows. For although the water was deep immediately below, huge holes being scoured out by the water falling through the lock, a little way downstream there was always an extensive bar of gravels thrown up by back currents. This is characteristic even of modern weirs. The barges then proceeded downstream on the slowly moving flash.

In Henley Town Hall hangs a copy of a finely-detailed painting by Jan Siberechts, *A View of Henley from the Wargrave Road*, dated about 1690. It is unique in showing a large Western barge passing downstream through Marsh flash lock, revealing that the process was perhaps only rarely as haphazard and dangerous as outlined above. Six crew members are at work at a large winch or capstan on the opposite bank about 110yds (100m) upstream, and have obviously let down the heavily laden barge slowly through the opening in the mill dam by means of a tow-line from the capstan to the stern of the barge. One man is on the stern of the barge in the narrow lock opening, another is ready to replace the lock tackle. The painting also depicts a string of laden pack mules passing along the deeply rutted road, reminding one of the poorer alternative to water transport which existed until comparatively recent times.

When the downward craft had passed, any waiting to proceed upstream were dragged through against the current by means of ropes attached to the capstan, which was sturdily constructed on a wooden staging above every flash lock. The rotting remains of the last Thames flash lock capstan may still be seen a short distance above Hurley weir. Much of it is buried in the ground but the massive centre post, with a circumference of 4ft 3in (130cm), still stands to a height of 6ft (180cm). The six beams against which the barge crews once strained are each 5ft 6in (168cm) long. The pulling rope would be brought from the barge and perhaps only a few turns taken around the base of the post – enough to give purchase – the slack being taken away as the post

9 Marlow mill dam in 1753. The thimble, corn and oil mills lie at the end of the incredibly long 'Ware' in which can be seen the posts of the flash lock. The huge capstan is built on a revetted platform opposite. The timber bridge crossed the river from the *Anglers* pub to St Peter Street

10 Marlow 'Ware' c. 1867. Old houses cluster at the foot of St Peter's Street by the site of the timber bridge. Barges are moored where the capstan stood

11 Marsh flash lock, c. 1690. Marsh and New Mills stood at either end of the dam. A barge with rounded bow, probably carrying sacks of malt, is being let down with a rope from the capstan to the left off the picture (Jan Siberechts, *A View of Henley*, detail)

turned. Needless to say, the men had to step over the rope as they circled. Although often augmented by men or horses on other tow-lines, capstans had to be immensely strong to draw up a laden barge against the current, and there is no doubt that underground the Hurley post is set deep in heavy timberwork. After the barges had passed the pivoted weir-walk was then closed back in against its stop, and the rymers and paddles replaced. The water levels in the reach would then gradually climb back up to that which was required by the miller to work his wheel efficiently, therefore allowing the upward-bound craft to proceed on their way. This might take several hours, depending on the capacity of the reach

and the amount of water coming down. During wet periods when there was a lot of water in the river the locks were left open, levels were almost equal on both sides, and vessels simply negotiated the narrow openings as best they could.

The numerous flash locks on the much narrower river above Oxford were nearly all an integral part of fish weirs, with very little fall through them. These were the full width of the river in two sections, one being flash lock, the other comprised of paddles, or larger gates, which were connected by chains to hand winches on the walkway. These could be replaced by basket or net traps when required, usually when eels were migrating downstream in the autumn. Apart from Monk Mill at Radcot (mentioned by Thacker) there were few attempts to establish cornmills on the main river above Oxford. The Roque map of 1761 shows a mill in the vicinity of Skinners Weir above Pinkhill, and there are ancient backwaters of possible leats at Buscot, and at the former Ridges Weir in the Parish of Fyfield –

which according to the *Victoria County History* had a mill in 1427.

THE BRAY DISPUTE

The first reference to a Thames 'lok', presumably a flash lock, is in 1253, in the account of a complaint by the river traders of the City of London who had refused to pay tolls to Godfrey de Lyston, Constable of Windsor Castle and Bailiff of the Royal Manors of Cookham and Bray, he having then 'arrested' their boats and goods. The account shows that, even though the river was the free 'King's Highway', the boatmen appeared to be paying tolls even for tying up to the bank, or else a wharfage toll is indicated. The previously unpublished account comes from the *Proceedings of the Kings Bench* in the 37th year of the reign of Henry III.[7] Part of it reads:

It was commanded to Godfrey de Lyston that he should cause to deliver the ships and chattels of the citizens of London arrested in the Braylok for custom and elsewhere in his bailiwick till the morrow of St Michael and that the

12 The site of the ancient flash lock at Benson, *c.* 1866. The pound lock gate beams can be seen beyond. Thacker records that at this time there were large holes in the gates and it took 40 minutes to work through

same Godfrey should then be before the Council of the Lord the King to show the rights of the King concerning the premises because the same citizens have made the Lord the King secure by Henry le Buscher and Reginald le Buscher that on that day they will be before the same Council of the Lord the King and will render to the Lord the King therefore what appertains to him of right.

And whereupon the Mayor and Bailiffs of London come and say that whereas they have always used such liberty that all their co-citizens of London whosoever having ships might freely go by water of Thames to carry Brushwood, Hay and other things that can be carried by ships by the aforesaid water the said Godfrey had arrested the ships of their co-citizens at the aforesaid place of Bray and takes distresses of them and exacts from each ship six pence contrary to their liberties.

And Godfrey comes and says for the King that he exacts nothing from them unjustly because the Lord the King is in seisin from all ships which pass through the water aforesaid and stay near the demesne of the Lord the King of Bray and fix a stake there or load there of six pence from every ship wether they be from London or from elsewhere but if they pass by the middle bed and proceed by the mid-stream of the Thames without making stay upon the Land of the Lord the King he will demand nothing of them and that the Lord the King has used such liberty. If it please the Lord the King and his Council he is quite willing that it be inquired of . . . .

In 1206 King John had given Bray mill and manor to Jordan of London. In a 1288 Inquisition in the Bray Court Rolls it was stated that Jordan and his heirs had rented the mill and several waters and stream of the same, plus islands, at 12 shillings a year. Jordan was called 'Atte Loke'. A Bray flash lock is not mentioned in later surveys. It was probably found unnecessary to dam completely the main river. An exceptionally long mill stream and adjacent barrier of several islands seems to have provided enough head of water to drive a small mill. Cookham was a similar case. The flash lock system persisted on the Thames until modern times and ended with the removal of Eaton Hastings Weir in 1937.

2 The Middles Ages

THE BUILDING TRADE

Traffic on the river continued to increase throughout the following centuries, and the obstructions and exactions grew also. In 1305 there is a winch and therefore a flash lock at Marlow, and in 1377 a 'new' lock at Hambleden. Further up river the powerful Knights Templars had erected a lock for their mills at Sandford, just below Oxford, and were doubtless charging well for the privilege of passing through; but the men of Oxford attached so much importance to their river trade that they took the law into their own hands and broke down the lock.

Bargemen were now paying tolls for passing under the early ramshackle wooden bridges, a penny pontage being charged at Maidenhead in 1337. Further charges at Staines, Windsor and Maidenhead brought complaints in 1376. These tolls were supposed to be used for the repair of the bridges, which could be damaged from time to time by heavy barges colliding with the piles, such as at Windsor in 1523, when Willaim Webbe was fined for 'brekyng ye leg of ye bridge'.[1] Further damage was caused by the continuous rubbing of heavy tow-lines, which wore into the bridge supports, but usually there were special guard piles at the navigation span around which the ropes could pass.

Despite the plagues which were to annihilate a third or more of the population, the middle of the fourteenth century brought a building boom of royal and ecclesiastical establishments all along the river. H. M. Colvin in *A History of the Kings Works* writes of timber carried by water from Byfleet to Wallingford Castle in 1343. Numerous stone barges made their ponderous way down to Wallingford and Windsor Castles with thousands of tons of Oxfordshire stone from Wheatley and Taynton quarries. In 1362 Edward III commissioned William

Coke of Wheatley to provide transport for stone for Windsor from Wheatley and Taynton 'both by land and water'. The Taynton stone was probably first laboriously transported overland by carts to Eynsham or possibly Radcot above Oxford, where it was loaded on to rafts or barges and sent down-river. Land transportation over the Chilterns to Henley was apparently necessary at times, but must have been extremely expensive. However, comparatively light goods could be carried quite cheaply. In 1338 part of the Oxfordshire wool production was collected at Oxford, carried to Henley overland and then shipped to London in 'shutes' at the low cost of sixpence a sarpler, estimated to be about one tenth of a penny per mile.[2]

It seems that the carts which were in general use in the fourteenth century could only carry a maximum load of about two tons and therefore specially built wagons may have been used to carry loads of up to five tons of building stone, when at least eight horses would have been required to haul over the unpaved 'ways' that existed then. The distance that such heavy loads could be moved was probably less than ten miles a day. On the other hand, a barge of the period may have carried 50 tons and travelled up to 30 miles a day.

In 1367 coal for the Windsor Castle forges was brought by sea from Newcastle to London, where it was transhipped into shutes for the Thames voyage. The Treasurer's Accounts of Abingdon Abbey for 1383 and 1384 include payments for freestone, ragstone and ashlar from Wheatley and Taynton, plus water carriage from 'Whatele', presumably Sandford, because the affluent abbey even spent the large sum of 5s 5d on an elaborate tunic for the Sandford boatman. One can imagine him in his new livery,

13 Caversham Bridge, *c.* 1865. This unique 'half and half' bridge lasted until 1869. The medieval stone arches were too small for barges and therefore the Reading portion had typical lower-Thames wooden spans for navigation

local man made good, yelling abuse at sweating labourers clinging to taut ropes as creaking wooden cranes swung blocks of masonry over his precious barges.[3]

In the fourteenth century the vast tile works at Penn in Buckinghamshire were turning out thousands upon thousands of roofing and ornamental floor tiles for churches, abbeys and castles. In 1356 alone, William of Wykeham, the clerk of works at Windsor, bought 41,000.[4] It was then that the tiny Parish of Hedsor benefitted from its geographical position, being situated on the great bend of the river where it runs closest to Penn. The tiles were carted from the works about six miles in a fairly direct southerly route – which can still be traced today across the higher country to the east of the

Wycombe Valley, to the top of the hill overlooking the river.

On the last half-mile of the route the heavily-laden carts or pack animals had to make their slippery way down a steep chalk ridge to Hedsor Wharf. Throughout the medieval period many other products such as corn and wood must have come out of Buckinghamshire via this ridge. Its soft chalk crown was slowly cut in two by thousands of sharp hooves, sliding logs and heavy wheels. The result is one of the deepest sunken trackways known in the area. Its estimated depth is 16ft (5m) and overall width 80ft (24m). This is on the line of the supposed Roman Road from St Albans to Silchester, where it may have crossed the Thames, but the evidence for this is scanty, the river at this point not being suitable for a crossing today. The 'Carte-Waye' leading down 'Woodcock Hill' is mentioned several times in sixteenth-century documents, being included in the leasehold of the Wharf. In the eighteenth century a charge of sixpence for all conveyances was taken at a toll bar at the top of the hill. This track, always the property of the Lords of

the Manor of Hedsor, finally went out of use in about 1850 after the closing of the wharf.[5]

In 1350 thousands of roof tiles, and the expert Bucks tylers to fit them, were sent to the Palace of Westminster. Many London churches also received fine decorated floor tiles. Buckinghamshire designs on tiles – recovered from Brooks Wharf, Queenhithe in 1867 – prove that some, if not all, came via the river. Floor tiles also went up the valley by cart or barge to Little Marlow Monastery, Hurley Priory, Reading Abbey, Wallingford Castle, Dorchester Abbey, Godstow Nunnery and New College, Oxford.

A few miles to the north-east of Hedsor there were medieval kilns situated on the good quality clays at Hedgerley, Fulmer and Chalfont, where a thousand years earlier dozens of primitive kilns were manufacturing Romano-British pottery. The most convenient trade route for the products of the area is not only by Hedsor Wharf but also through the gap in the chalk cliffs just downstream on the Cliveden Estate. Here lies a so-called ancient packway which has long been thought of as being on the line of a

14 Cookham Bridge, *c.* 1910. A downstream view of the old navigable Hedsor channel which follows the line of the polled willows round Sashes Island, towards Cliveden. 'The Carteway' leads from the top left down to Hedsor Wharf. A weir now blocks the channel and craft proceed to the right via the lock cut

route to the west from London, which, prior to the thirteenth-century Maidenhead bridge, crossed the river at My Lady Ferry. However, this is clearly a strange route for such a road which, if such roads existed at this time, more likely always took a route through Maidenhead or even further to the south over much flatter country. Perhaps large-scale excavations on the beautiful riverside lawns of Cliveden will produce signs of a wharf and many examples of goods from the Buckinghamshire kilns, from Roman pottery to medieval decorated floor tiles.

Edward III was soon receiving many home comforts by water at his new apartments at Windsor, particularly ale, which on one occasion in 1386 was brought by a bargemaster with the fascinating name of William Shrympelmershe, who was tried (and

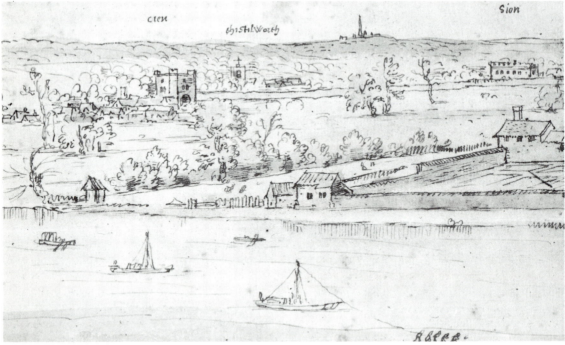

15 Hedsor Wharf, 1834. The Tudor wharf house and barge horse stables stand close to the water. (W. Tombleson)

16 Detail from a view of Richmond palace, 1562. The earliest known view of swimhead Western barges, one being towed upstream by five halers (Anthony Van Den Wynegaerde). *Ashmolean Museum, Oxford*

acquitted) because one of his bargehands was drowned on the journey.[6] A similar accident five years later on a 'lyghter' laden with wine and other luxuries resulted in the confiscation of the vessel under the law of deodand, by which an inanimate object which caused death was forfeit to the Crown.

Each succeeding monarch repeated the earlier laws which attempted to control the erection of weirs (probably those primarily for trapping fish), but the flash lock system was well established and vital for mills and navigation. The interference of the natural flow of the river by the weirs had caused shallows in many places and, ironically, the flash locks were now essential to give a flash of water to carry craft over the shoals. Thus, in 1403 Sir John Drayton of Rotherfield Peppard was indicted for not keeping his lock and winches in good repair. This was probably at Marsh, near Henley. Tolls at the flash locks, bridges and wharfs were now making steady profit for their owners, usually the lords of the manors or the local abbot; even the boats of the merchant guild of Reading had to pay the abbey a toll of one penny each way at 'Brockenburgh Lok' to get to the town wharf on the river Kennet. Strangers had to pay double! But sometimes the King granted concessions to towns so that they could continue their trade with as little harassment as possible. In 1459 the small manor of Wooburn in Buckinghamshire was granted freedom of access to its wharf and exemption from tolls and customs payable to the Crown on goods to and from the wharf and from obligatory conveyance of goods for the King's use.

The carriage of building stone continued throughout the fifteenth century, notably to Westminster, the Royal House at Sheen, for the building of the royal chapel at Windsor and also for Eton College. In the latter case it was thought necessary to take Headington stone overland to Culham, and later even as far as Henley, before it was put on to barges. H. M. Colvin states that in 1448 Roger Keys, Master of the Works, had inspected the river between Abingdon and Eton from a barge, which seems to prove that Henley was not head of navigation as has been suggested. The task occupied him for eight days and, owing to weirs and other obstructions, it did not prove satisfactory. Any number of factors may have influenced this decision. An often quoted cause of navigational hazards are the fish weirs. These were lightly-built structures which mostly did

not span the entire channel – at least below Oxford – and it is unlikely that they could obstruct a heavy barge, particularly one under His Majesty's authority. It is also unlikely that there were more mill dams than recorded in later surveys. It may have been that there was a prolonged drought or that the only craft available were deep-draughted vessels from tidal waters which had an excessive draught for the upper river when laden with stone.

In the latter half of the fifteenth century, letters from London received by wool merchant Sir William Stonor of Stonor House near Henley show that there was a regular delivery service from Queenhithe by bargemaster William Somer, who brought many domestic items to Henley wharf, including dried and salted fish, hogsheads of wine, spices, glassware and even a silk gown for Lady Stonor.[7] Other clients may have received similar goods at wharfs on the way up. The voyage from London usually took five days. Somers may have returned to London with country produce, including wool for export to Calais. Queenhithe lay almost in the shadow of St Paul's Cathedral, and for centuries served as the main London wharf for the barges trading from the West Country, which meant anywhere above London Bridge. Stow, in his *Survey of London*, states there was a market here in 1302, corn being one of the principle commodities landed in 1592. Later, Defoe speaks of one hundred ton barges landing meal and malt.

In the sixteenth century building stone was coming upstream from Surrey and imported from Caen, but local materials were used whenever possible, including timber from the Chilterns and Windsor forest and flint from chalk quarries such as at Little Marlow, where the King's carts damaged the crops of the local nunnery. In the 1530s the rebuilding of Hampton Court Palace brought down bricks from Taplow as well as stone from the Cotswolds. The demand for timber for houses and ships brought increasing destruction to the ancient forests which still clothed many parts of the country at this time. Oak was particularly useful, and much of it came out of the great forest of Windsor. In about 1535 the Bishop of Winchester sold large quantities of timber from the estate of Billingbear in the heart of the Windsor oak forest.[8] It was shipped from Water Oakley near Bray, where a timber wharf had stood from at least 1333. There was another wharf at

Maidenhead, of which in 1530 that great traveller Leland said, 'There is a great wharfeage of timbre and fier wood on the west end of the bridge and this wood cummith out of Berkshir, and the great woddis of the forest of Windelsore, and the Greath Frithe.' In 1555 barges were carrying stone from Reading Abbey and lead from Abingdon and Wallingford to Windsor for the construction of the five mile conduit from Winkfield which carried water to the Castle.

It was not all work on the river. In *An Eye on the Thames* Alan Wykes states that in 1555 William and Elizabeth Bates of Abingdon organized a pleasure cruise to Oxford on a ribbon-bedecked boat furnished with amusements, card games, liquor and pies. The trippers were to see one particular spectacle

17 Windsor Castle, *c.* 1708. Much of the castle was built with stone brought by water. Three laden swimhead barges sail downstream with the prevailing wind. Another is towed upstream by five horses who have to swim the river at both ends of Romney Island (Leonard Knyff). *Reproduced by Gracious Permission of Her Majesty The Queen*

in front of Balliol College – the burning of Protestant Bishops Hugh Latimer and Nicholas Ridley. Unfortunately Mr Wykes cannot give the source of this material.

NAVIGATION TO OXFORD

There has been much speculation about the absence of records for upstream traffic to Oxford during the Middle Ages. Oxford historians have stated that barges could not reach that far because the river below was blocked or at least in a bad state of repair. Some claim that Henley was the head of navigation, but there are a number of records for traffic above Henley at this time, as demonstrated above. Anyone who has actually looked at the river above Henley can see that, apart from during severe drought, it is impossible to block it, and obviously there was generally sufficient depth for at least shallow-draughted craft, if required. Thames bargemen were just as resourceful as their River Severn counterparts, who had to contend with far shallower waters at times. Oxford itself, however, had declined drastically as a trading centre during the plague years and

was now catering mainly for scholars, so it was probably thought not worth while taking a big trading barge there. Dr Prior in the excellent book *Fisher Row* quotes from the accounts of merchant Thomas West of Wallingford who writes that in 1567 his barge was held up at Caversham because his winch was broken. She therefore surmises that the river had so declined that bargemen had to provide their own portable winches to get through some flash locks.[9] However, the winch in question was much more likely to have been the standard barrel windlass on the bow of the barge, used mainly for raising and lowering the mast.

West had a half share in a barge, probably the *Mary Grace*. His downward trade was chiefly in firewood, timber, corn and malt. Upstream came cargoes such as wine, salted and dried fish and particularly coal, which had been brought to London by ship from Newcastle. It appears that his barge went no further upstream that Sutton Courtenay and Culham wharfs; coal for the Oxford area was unloaded at Burcot.[10] Several factors may have stopped barges from proceeding to Oxford: their size, lack of orders, or the cost of tolls at the upper flash locks exceeding that of carting goods on the comparatively short overland route from Burcot wharf. Flash locks were recorded at the mills from Sutton to Iffley in Bishop's 1585 survey – and certainly hadn't appeared overnight. The lock at Nuneham was one of only a very few below Oxford that had no attendant mill, but was probably mainly a fish weir which also helped to increase water levels up to Sandford.

The trouble with the 13 miles or so below Oxford for deeply-laden craft from London was that, for geological reasons, the channel did not naturally retain a good head of water. The fall of the land is much steeper here than on the rest of the navigable river. Therefore the millers had to build higher dams on this section, which at times proved too difficult and expensive for large barges to negotiate. Today there are five locks on this stretch with a total fall of 30ft (9m), giving an average fall per mile of about 28in (70cm); Sandford and Culham being the deep-

18 A view of Henley (detail) *c.* 1690. The painting is full of valuable detail. The rutted Wargrave road approaches the original wooden bridge. A barge goes downstream under sail and oar and others wait at the wharf for loads of Chiltern timber (Jan Siberechts)

est on the non-tidal river. The lock fall for the equivalent distance below that is only 12in (30cm) per mile and above Oxford about 18in (45cm) per mile.

Although there may have been few large long-distance craft above Burcot at this time, there were probably many unrecorded small local barges and working punts carrying cereals for the mills – and fishing, farming and market produce between town, village and countryside.

JOHN BISHOP

Any overall description of the river up to the sixteenth century must be mainly based on supposition, so it is with relief that the date of 1579 is reached, when we have the first known survey which can be relied upon to give a few reasonably authentic statistics. The description, in the Strype edition of Stow's *Survey of London*, states that there were 23 locks, 16 mills, 16 flood gates and seven weirs between Maidenhead and Oxford. It seems that out of the 23 flash locks, seven were apart from any attendant mill, and were incorporated into seven weirs, which were probably fishing weirs, or were specially erected to take craft over particularly shallow reaches. At each mill there was a floodgate, or more likely several gates or 'bucks', or paddle-and-rymer tackle. In 1580 John Bishop, who must have had a considerable interest in the Thames trade, complained to the Lord Treasurer that the locks and weirs were causing considerable havoc to barge traffic. He gives the total number of weirs on the river as over 70. This figure must include the whole river, including the tideway, where Her Majesty had a few little domestic fish weirs of her own. Many flash locks had been so increased in height that 'The going up the locks were so steep that every year cables had been broken that cost £400 and bargemen and goods drowned, and in coming down, the water fell so high that it sank the vessels and destroyed corn and malt wherewith they were laden.' In 1585 Bishop again attacked the flash lock

19 Whitchurch mill dam, 1793. The mill lies to the left. The flash lock is to the right of the islands with the capstan on the point of land above it. The towpath has timber revetment to stop erosion and provide moorings for the work punts, convenient for the pub just out of view! (J. Farington). See the Thames Conservancy Map in Volume I of *Thames Highway*

owners in a long complaint in verse, directed to the Queen. One of the worst locks seems to have been at Marlow, of which he says:

One Ffarmer hath a lock in store
That hath made many a child to weep
Their mothers beg from dore to dore
Their Ffathers drowned in the deep

At Ffarmers lock foure men be loste
Of late I putt you out of doubt
Three were drowned the stream them toste
The fourth he had his braines knocked out.

Bishop's outburst was answered in a more reasonable manner in a petition from 'those concerned in these locks, wears and mills'. The reasons given for retaining the flash locks were as follows:

(1) That the mills and locks were of as great antiquity as the towns and villages to which they adjoin: That they were a necessity for grinding corn and for the passage of barges: That within the banks and weirs there were infinite loads of chalk and rubbish, which if loosed would be the best way to choke the river.

(2) The causes of the increased peril of the passage was that the barges were now of a greater burden; almost double what they used to be; that the bargemen loaded them beyond reason. They used to partly unload below the lock and reship again above, even when they had but seven or eight loads. Now they came with 20 loads they would unload nothing. They employed people of no skill, and travelled so late and so early as to be unable to see what they were doing, and they travelled on a Sunday as well as every other day. It was likely that there would be more accidents as the number of barges had increased from 10 or 12 to 80.

(3) Touching the accidents at Marlow, one was drowned by manifest negligence, partly that the barge was overloaded, partly that it wanted washboards on the sides. Another was drowned, but not at the lock, and another by his own negligence. Another came up the lock in winter so late that he could not discern what he did. It was no wonder that the cables parted, they were made of ill stuff, and the barges so great and so heavily laden.

Bishop submitted lists of the locks and weirs with his complaints. The 1585 list beginning:

1. Rea lock belonging to Harry Merrye, one of the

20 Maidenhead timber wharf, 1749. A rather fanciful view upstream towards Ray and Taplow Mills and the Cliveden escarpment. Cliveden house has been moved a mile downstream! (Artist unknown)

yeomen of Her Majesties chamber and in the keeping of Robert Weston.

2.   One weir called Hedgeworth's Weir belonging to Hughe Cottrell, in the parish of Cowcombe. (Cookham).

3.   Marlowe locks belonging to Thomas (Far)mer, gent., and kept by George Westcotte. The lock in the parish of Byssham, the mill and flood gate in Great Marlow.

We see that the early 'lok' at Bray had now apparently gone, and Ray flash lock at Maidenhead was now the first major obstruction upstream from London. Cookham had only a fishing weir, 'Hedgeworth's', possibly a corruption of Hedsor, in the vicinity of Sashes Island. Marlow flash lock was situated directly on the site of the floodgates of the modern weir, typical of many others. The full list of flash locks on the river will not be repeated here. Thacker has adequately covered this, later surveys, and legislation, in his standard work, *Thames Highway*.

3 The Western barge

BARGE EVOLUTION

What were the barges like which had been using the river up until this time; how were they worked and what were the crews like? These inland craft had developed differently to the coastal craft of Britain, where the traditional clinker hull design and square sail of the Viking long-ship survived for centuries, after most other material remnants of that culture had been lost for ever. The basic design lived on in many types of coastal craft in various parts of Britain. Clinker hulls, with overlapping strakes, tapering to a point at bow and stern, could still be seen on London River in the eighteenth century, although in many cases the square sail had given way to fore and aft rig more suitable for coastal work. On the other hand, the great keels of the east-coast rivers retained the square-rigged sail up to the twentieth century – but in this case the deep sturdy hulls came to be sometimes carvel-built. On the River Severn the graceful trow also became carvel built and developed a 'D' shaped transom stern. The larger trows adopted fore-and-aft rig in the eighteenth century but the smaller versions which were designed for inland work, including the Thames and Severn Canal route, in many cases retained a square-rigged sail.

Many different types of working barge evolved, the Severn trow, Humber and Tyne keels, billy boy, luff barge and hoy, from which eventually developed the famous Thames and Medway spritsail barges. They all had two things in common, they were all built with reasonable freeboard to withstand a certain amount of rough water when sailing on wide estuaries or coastal waters, and were all flat-bottomed so that they could negotiate the shallowest

inlets and rivers, and could be beached to take on a cargo on any shore. Similarly-designed working craft from the Continent, particularly Dutch schuyts, were a common sight in the Port of London throughout the centuries. Many traded far upstream, catching or buying eels and lampreys which were used as sea-fishing bait.

Some of the earliest inland river craft were probably no more than simple rafts which were undoubtedly used to ferry stock and fodder across from bank to bank and even carry heavy goods downstream, but they would have been too ungainly to have been used for long distance work. A working boat navigating solely on inland waters does not require a great amount of freeboard to withstand heavy seas. It must be stable, flat-bottomed for shallow waters, of massive construction to withstand rough usage at wharfs or the inevitable battering from obstructions on the riverbed, and also be simple and cheap to build. All these requirements are fulfilled in the simple working punt, or 'flat', which is still used today for maintenance work and which has a history going back into the depths of time, not only on the Thames but on other working rivers in England and Western Europe.

On the Thames, the term Western barge meant any commercial barge which traded only inland, westwards of London Bridge. So far there have been no buried wrecks of medieval or earlier barges excavated from the upper Thames, and one can only make educated guesses as to what these inland trading craft looked like; their builders left no specifications or drawings for later historians to study. What were the origins of these barges? Like many other so-called primitive craft they had been

21 Remenham, 1811. A barge heavily laden with sacks of malt is towed downstream past Temple Island, now the start of Henley Regatta course. What appears to be a set-pole is being used as a towing mast. Havell drew barges with stern windlasses which is certainly untypical. (W. Havell)

born in prehistoric times, and as their trade was on shallow inland waters there were definite limitations on their size and, therefore, never any need to alter much their early basic design.

CELTIC CRAFT

Many different kinds of wooden craft came into being in prehistoric times, mostly developed from dugout canoes or logboats. According to present archaeological evidence, in Western Europe the dugout was being used in the Bronze Age, and in many places, including Britain, lasted almost into modern times. Plank-built craft were also being developed at an early date on inland waters, and it seems that from about 500 BC one European method to make larger craft was to expand square-sectioned

punt-like dugouts by splitting them longitudinally and inserting planks between the two halves. Therefore, in the Iron Age, there arose a 'Celtic' or Western European tradition of boat and ship building, which differed in a number of ways from the Scandinavian craft made with keel-planks and overlapping strakes (clinker-built), and the Mediterranean rounded carvel (butted planks) construction with mortices, tenons and dowels (treenails).[1]

On the continent by the second century AD, because of the requirements of a sophisticated Roman trading network, it was found necessary to build large craft for the carriage of heavy goods along shallow rivers. The native craftsmen had limitless experience in building timber houses, forts, carts and even large ships, which had astonished Julius Caesar when he came up against the Venetic fleet off the coast of Brittany. It is tempting to think that migrating Iron Age tribes crossed over to Britain from Brittany and perhaps the Rhine Delta

22 Zwammerdam barge 6, built 1800 years ago. The construction closely resembles later Thames barges

23   Walton, 1811. The ferry punt and swimhead barge have many features in common with Celtic craft. (W. B. and C. Cooke)

in craft very much like these.

The barge builders provided the required river craft for their Roman masters by using the expanded dugout principle on a massive scale, using six or seven large oak strakes to form the flat bottom of the craft, and finishing off on each side with the 'L'-shaped chine strakes which resulted from the split dugouts. Further planks were used to bring the craft to the required length, and additional ones some-times fixed to the top of the chine plank for extra depth. Some barges received no longitudinal strength from any keel or keelson timber running along the centre of the bed of the craft; much of the strength of these barges came from the chine plank. The bottom planks were sometimes joined Roman style with mortise-and-tenon joints, fixed by dow-els, but very often a particular Celtic method was used in which the strakes were held to numerous ribs by driving large iron nails right through, clenching them over and driving the points back in. Knees were extensively used to strengthen the sides. Both

ends of the barges gradually rose up into a 'swim-head' by using scarfed planks.

The overall plan of most of these barges was a long rectangle, sometimes narrowing towards bow and stern. The largest so far discovered, from a spectacular excavation at an ancient Roman inland port of Zwammerdam near Rotterdam, was 112ft (34m) in length, nearly as long, although somewhat narrower, than the largest eighteenth-century Thames barges. Mast steps were found on some barges, but it is not known if these craft were sailed or towed from the bank.[2]

Several barge wrecks of Romano-British date have been found in the bed of London River and perhaps two of them provide some further evidence to the origins of Thames Western barges. They were both of oak carvel construction bearing some features identical to the Rhine barges. The timbers were massive and held to the ribs with clenched iron nails, and the seams sometimes caulked with hazel twigs. The small dumpy second-century AD sailing barge excavated at Blackfriars in 1962 was found to have been carrying Kentish ragstone from the Med-way area. She was about 50ft (15m) in length, 19ft (6m) in beam, decked, and with a good freeboard for estuary work.[3] Another craft of similar date was found in 1958 on a side stream underneath of the site of part of Guys Hospital in Bermondsey. It was also about 50ft (15m) in length but narrower, with a beam of about 14ft (4.5m), and with much less freeboard, suitable only for river work.

Unfortunately, none of the British craft had the square section punt-like shape of some of the European craft such as from Zwammerdam in Holland and Pommeroeul on a Rhine tributary in Belgium, which have an uncanny resemblance to illustrations of later Thames barges and work punts, so the Celtic link cannot be ignored. The design fulfilled the requirements of many generations of Thames bargemen, who may have carried on the ancient traditions after the departure of the Romans, and on through the Dark Ages into the settlement of the English. If *Aldershot*, one of the last Basingstoke Canal barges, had been left to sink into the bottom of the canal instead of being burnt in 1984, archaeologists of the future would have found she was held together with clenched iron nails!

BARGE ETYMOLOGY

Some of the first medieval references to trading craft on the freshwater Thames include 'ships' from London in 1205 and 1253 and a 'lyghter' laden with wine and other goods proceeding to Windsor in 1391.

The term 'barge' seems to have been generally adopted in the fifteenth century. Thacker quotes an Act of Edward I in 1274 which mentions 'ships and great barges' between London and Oxford, although it is not known if the translation is correct, as no reference is given. The *Oxford English Dictionary* states that the term, possibly derived from the Latin 'barga', was first used in England for small sea-going sailing craft, and attributes the first mention of 'barges' on inland waters to Caxton in 1480. However, the London to Henley trade by William Somer and his barge is mentioned several times in the Stonor family letters in 1476.

A possibly far more ancient term than barge is 'shout'. In 1356 there were complaints that the quay at Baynards Castle in London had been enlarged 'to the nuisance of ships, shouts and boats'.[4] Thacker quotes a petition of 1376 from the King's subjects who had shouts on the upper river. The O.E.D.'s first reference is for 1395, with a quote regarding 'mariners called Shoutemen'.

In 1403 Sir John Drayton was indicted for not maintaining his flash lock on the Thames in the Manor of Rotherfield Peppard (now Marsh lock above Henley). The translation by Anthony Wood, the seventeenth-century Oxford historian, continues with 'for the necessary conduct of barges and shoules', which is obviously a mis-translation of shoutes.[5] F. G. G. Carr in *Sailing Barges* quotes an incident in 1414, when a schoute laden with building stone was sunk while negotiating London Bridge.

Yet another reference, unfortunately undated, comes from the 1839 *Chronicles of London Bridge* in which the anonymous author quotes from an apparently fifteenth-century bridge estates survey, in which the resident sheuteman was provided with dry accommodation on the bridge where, because of the fluctuating tides, he and his men could often be out on the river at night in all weathers, maintaining the bridge-works against emergencies, man-made or natural.

There are no known later references to the name on the Thames. The conclusion is that 'shout' could mean anything from a large up-river trading craft to a maintenance boat. In other words, an earlier or alternative name for a barge. Only the Rotherfield Peppard reference seems to make a distinction between a barge and a shout. In the Lincolnshire Fens the term continued into the eighteenth century, meaning a small flat-bottomed market or eel fishing boat, and was obviously closely allied to that used for the Dutch flat-bottomed spritsail eel boat, the schuyt, a craft often seen on London River up until the 1930s. It is tempting to wonder if the name was originally introduced to the Thames by boatmen of the late Iron Age when they may have first brought their flat-bottomed Celtic river-craft building techniques from the Rhine delta in what is now Holland.

The original term 'Western' barge, first recorded in 1548[6] and meaning those craft trading westwards of London Bridge, had by the eighteenth century been turned into 'West Country'. While we now think of Devon and Cornwall as the West Country, at that time a citizen of London would have thought that Maidenhead or Windsor were in the remote west.

BARGE DESIGN

Many paintings and prints of the river from the sixteenth century onwards depict Western barges, and from their study it is possible to build up a fairly

24 Sutton Courtenay, 1928. A Thames Conservancy gang with maintenance flats working to remove a fallen willow. (*Oxford Journal Illustrated*)

accurate idea of how they were constructed and operated, always remembering that the artist was most often concerned with a picturesque scene and often only drew barges to create extra interest and movement. There was a great variation in style, technical ability and understanding of the subject in view. Some artists had their own favourite idea of what a barge should look like and one sometimes sees some strange interpretations! But fortunately most seem to depict faithfully the various styles of barges which changed through time and from lower to upper river.

The illustrations from the late sixteenth century to the beginning of the nineteenth almost invariably show large punt-shaped, largely un-decked craft, with very little freeboard when laden with various cargoes of filled sacks, barrels, timber, hay or straw.

Some have a stemmed, rounded bow, but an equal number are swim-headed like the Celtic barges, with the flat bottom rising to a square-cut, partly-decked bow. Sometimes there is a slight narrowing of the hull and an upward sweep or sheer of the gunwales as they approach the swimhead. Both types had budgett sterns, square and undercut, with a deadwood, from which hung a huge wooden rudder. This could not be very deep (otherwise it would foul the riverbed) and was therefore very long to allow some steerage at a slow speed.

Some of the largest barges, which in the eighteenth century were said to carry up to two hundred tons, had a draught of only 4ft (1.20m) laden, achieved because of the flat bottom and great length. Their beam was comparatively narrow and most averaged a length to beam ratio of 6 or 7 to 1, very similar proportions to an ordinary fishing punt and the earlier Celtic craft. The largest barges capable of going as far upstream as Wallingford had a length of about 128ft (39m) and a beam of about 20ft (6m),

25 Swimheads and budgett sterns, 1802. In the foreground is a tideway hoy. To its right is a Western barge showing the iron hoops of the awning. Above are River Lee barges. (W. H. Pyne)

26 Medmenham Ferry, c. 1890. The punt shape provides an ideal stable platform for heavy loads. Many Thames ferries were pulled across on a wire rope running through rollers. The carter and ferryman seem to have just returned from the Boer War!

27 A modern steel swimhead ballast punt, originally used for shoal dredging. Dimensions of two metres by ten metres and loading about five tons

carrying 170 tons, to Oxford 88ft (26m) × 17ft (5m), carrying one hundred tons, and to Lechlade, 88ft (26m) × 11ft 9in (3.58m) carrying 65 tons. Westwards from Lechlade, barges of six or seven tons went as far as Cricklade, where today it is unusual to see anything larger than a canoe. Some modern writers say that Waterhay Bridge was once the head of commercial navigation, a statement hard to accept by anyone who has navigated, or rather scrambled, along those last few shallow, twisting miles above Cricklade.

Barges were built at small slipways throughout the length of the river, very likely in open situations similar to the Suffolk Stour barge depicted in one of John Constable's famous paintings. The bottom was usually made of elm and the sides of oak. A complete list of materials for a barge 'in the Experiment Form' is given in Samuel Bird's estimate of 1791 in Appendix I of Humphrey Household's *Thames and Severn Canal*. Although keel-less, there must have been a keelson and possibly even side-keelsons running the

length of the bottom to provide very necessary longitudinal strength. There would be numerous oak frames holding the bottom planks together, and knees to join the vertical sides to the bottom at the chine, and a ceiling or floor of timbers to protect the hull from damage by heavy cargoes. The sides also may have been double-skinned like some later barges.

The so-called primitive shape of the punt-like, swim-headed, Western barge, hides the fact that the builders, particularly of the larger ones, exercised great skill in design and construction techniques to produce such a long and narrow craft, capable of carrying up to two hundred tons. Some features of design can only be guessed at. For instance, there must have been crossbeams at intervals at gunwale height to provide some rigidity to the otherwise flexible sides of such a completely undecked craft. Tension chains may also have run along the beams from wale to wale to stop the sides from spreading, a necessary requirement for some later barges and narrow boats. A very strong sailing beam and mast-case was also required where tall masts were used, to cope with the enormous stresses when under sail or on tow.

4 The work of the bargemen

MAST AND SAIL

The economics of building and maintaining early Thames trading barges, and employing the crews to man them, are little understood. Every barge had a master who was also called the cost-bearer, responsible for paying tolls and providing for the crew. The master may have owned and ran his own vessel or may have been employed by local merchants who had shares in a barge. Some merchants may have owned several barges and, as trade grew, opened up barge-building yards to cater for others. Barges each had their own port of origin, and probably operated mainly for their own local town wharfinger, crews returning to homes and families while waiting for the next cargo. Some may have been part-time bargemen, working on the land when river trade was slack.

Barge crews were said to consist of up to six men and a boy. Some illustrators depict women on board, but it is not known if this was mere artistic licence of whether families travelled together. On local trading barges, particularly in the London area, there was apparently no shelter for the crew at all and they probably slept ashore at night. Some seventeenth-century illustrations of Windsor Castle depict small barges on the foreshore, with temporary tent-like awnings over the aft section. But for long distance voyages to Oxford and beyond, which might take weeks in adverse conditions, shelter was provided by a large canvas tilt or awning supported on iron hoops across the stern. This may even have been the only home for some bargemen. A hearth of brick or clay was a necessity for warmth and cooking, and beds were probably straw-filled mattresses. When the barge was filled with a bulky cargo, access

from one end to the other was by a wide gunwale, possibly provided with transverse ridges as footholds for when the crew were shoving the barge with poles.

Every barge was equipped with a single mast, possibly stepped loosely into a lutchett box or mast-case for easy removal, or in a tabernacle, when the foot of the mast – particularly the very tall ones – may have been pivoted and counter-balanced. The mast was positioned slightly forward of centre, the most efficient position when single square-rigged sails were used. Three or four supporting shrouds ran from the masthead to each gunwale, just aft of the mast foot. These provided support when the mast was under strain when sailing or towing. Back-stays are sometimes shown when the barge has no stern awning, but never when there is one.

Forward, the mast was held upright with a fore-stay from masthead to stayfall tackle at the bow, the mast being raised and lowered with a wooden barrel side-pawl windlass on the small foredeck. The windlass was fixed to a pair of heavy wooden 'bits' which passed through the deck on to the floor timbers. The tops of the bits stood higher than the windlass, and were shaped to leave twin stubs for tying or checking ropes. The windlass was probably of a simple hand-spike design on early craft but later, as masts grew higher and heavier, iron gearing, ruffles and pawls, and winding handles were incorporated.

A lowering mast was of course essential to negotiate low bridges. It must have been a quick and simple job when under sail to drop the single yard, loose the forestay, and let the mast fall back under its own weight on to a prop. Once the bridge had been shot, several crew members would make short work

28   Small barges below Windsor Castle, *c.* 1680. One craft has its cargo covered by a rain-proof sheet, another waits for passengers or freight, loaded via a gang-plank over the bow. (Jan Wyck)

of raising the mast again, especially if it was counter-balanced in the tabernacle. There would be a similar procedure when under tow. In this case, the towline had to be dropped and collected again on the other side of the bridge. Going downstream the barge simply shot the bridge, but against the current it had to be rowed through using very long oars called sweeps, or poled or quanted through using the craft's complement of set-poles.

Contemporary illustrations suggest that before fore-and-aft rig and spritsails started to appear on Western barges in the nineteenth century, single Viking style square-rigged sails were used almost universally on the larger craft. Although all roughly rectangular in shape, they varied considerably in dimensions, some being tall and narrow, others being much wider than the beam of the barge. The predominant colour was tan, probably from the traditional preservative treatment later used on the Thames and Medway spritsail barges. Mixtures included horse fat, linseed and cod oil, red and yellow ochres and water. A low, single square sail is not very efficient when close-hauled and the narrowness of the Thames allowed very little leeway drift, and therefore early barges with such sails only set them when the wind was mainly from astern. On the Thames that meant the prevailing west wind came in very handy on the downstream voyage, as much of the river runs roughly west to east. When going upstream, wind and current generally combined against the use of sail, and towing was mainly employed.

During the eighteenth century, if not earlier, some larger barges, particularly on the lower river, were equiped with incredibly tall and comparatively narrow square-rigged sails. In spite of its apparently awkward appearance, a sail of this type was extremely efficient, providing a long flat aerofoil shape with an extensive 'leading edge'. This would give maximum 'lift' when the yard was braced round to the wind, and draw the barge along when going to windward.[1]

In spite of the height of the sail, a very low centre of gravity meant that barges were unlikely to suffer unduly from heeling in high winds. The rig did not make the barge fast, nor necessarily allow it to sail very close to the wind; Western barge hulls were not

29 Windsor Bridge, 1793. A large Western barge with a short towing mast lies anchored by set-poles. Square and sprit-rigged barges cluster round the bridge. (J. Farington)

30 Shooting Windsor Bridge. Two men are lowering the gear with the windlass, another is propelling the barge with a sweep. (Date and artist unknown)

31   A View on the Thames, 1789. A deeply laden barge equipped with the ultimate in tall narrow sails. (William Marlow)

built for speed nor fitted with leeboards to stop sideways drift. But it did provide the most efficient form of propulsion when the wind was in the right quarter and there was no strong current to fight against.

The top edge of the sail was securely bent to the yard, which at its centre was loosely fixed to the mast by a bead parrel or iron traveller, so that it could easily be hauled up and down by means of a halyard through a block near the top of the mast. The comparatively large number of crew members may have been able to raise yard and sail without mechanical assistance, but on the largest barges small halyard winches fixed to the mast case may have been used. Winches were probably not needed to adjust the sheets and braces controlling the sail. Some illustrations appear to show that when the barge was at rest, sail could be taken in without lowering the yard by roughly hauling up the foot of the sail to the yard with a buntline. Apart from the sail dimensions there was nothing particularly unique about this single square-rigged arrangement. It had originated on the Viking longships and continued into the twentieth century on the Humber keels, where wire and winches had replaced hemp rope and sheer muscle power.

SWEEPS AND SET-POLES

Sweeps have already been mentioned, being used to good effect when necessary. A pair could be fixed between thole pins on either gunwale towards the bows. At least one man would be needed for each sweep, rowing from a standing position, as Thames lightermen do.

Some of the most essential pieces of equipment on board were a number of long poles called set-poles. On the tideway spritsail barges, similar tools are called 'setting booms' and on the Norfolk wherries 'quant-poles'. Some modern Thames writers refer to them as 'ryepecks', which upper Thames bargemen

32   Eton College, *c.* 1777. A barge laden with timber. One of the few illustrations showing yard braces. (After Paul Sandby)

33   Low tide at Putney Bridge, 1793. A rare picture of a square-rigged barge close-hauled (sheets running forward and aft of the mast). The men in the foreground are long-netting for salmon. (J. Farington)

say is incorrect. This term should be reserved for the light, single-spiked iron-shod temporary mooring posts for fishing punts and other small craft.

Set-poles were usually made of ash and from about 14ft (4.5m) to 19ft (6m) in length. They were used, 'with incredible dexterity', to keep the barge away from shoals and obstructions, especially when passing through flash locks, and for moving the barge when other means were impractical. Bargemen would take a pole to the bows, thrust it down to the riverbed, and, by leaning on the pole and walking aft along the gunwale or a narrow sidedeck, would push the barge forward. To help with this, the poles had a 'T' shaped top to fit the bargeman's shoulder, the equivalent of the Norfolk quant button top. The bottom of the poles were shod with heavy iron 'V' shaped shoes to grip the riverbed. They had to be of considerable weight to

counteract the natural buoyancy of the very long poles.

Western barges do not appear to have used conventional anchors, but illustrations show that they were anchored when necessary by set-poles which were thrust down on to the riverbed on either side and lashed to convenient cleats on the gunwale. Bargemen were using identical equipment on the Rhine tributaries in Roman times. Several iron 'V' shaped shoes for barge poles, together with boat hooks and ryepeck points, were found by archaeologists in 1975 with second-century A.D. barges and logboats at the Roman river port at Pommeroeul in Belgium. Set-poles are still used by dredger crews on the upper Thames today.

The whole business of working manually a hundred-ton barge on a narrow river can only really be appreciated by practical experience – which is difficult to obtain today. It is possible to feel the exhilaration of a barge under sail by chartering a lower Thames spritsail barge – and aboard the two restored sailing Humber keels, the last Norfolk

34 Iron implements dredged from the river and restored. From the left; a set-pole, rypeck and large boat hook

wherry, or the last Tamar barge. Perhaps the last Severn trow will also be restored. Unfortunately, the old type of square-rigged Western barges vanished about 150 years ago, and the different techniques and problems involved in navigating them on an unpredictable river can only be imagined. It would be an interesting project to provide at least one of the small work punts which are still around with mast, sail and other necessary equipment, including a willing crew, and experiment. Unfortunately there are now no flash locks to work through.

HALING

A number of Roman monumental carvings graphically depict laden river barges being towed from the banks by gangs of men, and in later centuries this was the most widely used method of moving cargoes along rivers and canals, although other beasts of burden sometimes replaced men. For one of the few detailed descriptions of the rigours of towing by

manpower we must turn to the River Wye, generally swifter than the Thames, although similar scenes must have occurred at Thames flash locks and bridges.

Charles Heath, writing in about 1800, stated that it required five men to pull an unladen barge from Brockweir to Monmouth but, when laden, 15 men were needed for every 25 tons carried. This equates well with numbers required on the Thames. Heath remarked:

The rapidity of the current in many places renders this employment a work of great labour, particularly in dry seasons. In passing the different weirs, they are then obliged to fall with all their force flat on the ground, which is done by the shout of 'Yo Ho!' in which position they continue for a short space, when, on another shout being given, they rise up and, securing their step, fall down

35 Henley Bridge, 1834. An 'improved' Kennet or Thames and Severn type barge with spritsail. Set-poles are being used vigorously to keep off the shallows. (W. Tombleson)

a second time, and so on till they gain a more peaceful and greater depth of water.

In about 1850, K. M. Pitt, Master at Monmouth School, wrote that on the Wye:

There were many barges continually at work, keel-less, flat-bottomed vessels of great dimensions drawing but little water. These were fitted with a tall mast which could be lowered by a small winch carried on the forward decking. The bow was bluff and the sides protected by tarpaulins, so that they could carry downstream in a freshet a load which allowed only a few inches of free-board. High up the mast was a block through which the tow-rope was run, the spare rope being coiled on the stern decking near the captain who steered. Coming upstream the barge was towed by five or six men; Each had a leather breast-strap with a small harness rope which he could attach to the tow-rope. The captain could pay out or shorten the length of tow-rope as required. The men attached themselves to the tow-line about five yards apart. Hauling a loaded barge up-stream was no light task and, at

36 Isleworth, *c.* 1779. Halers tow a barge upstream on an embanked towpath. Each has a breast strap attached to the main cable. (Print from *The Modern British Traveller*)

a rapid, it was desperate work, the advance being only foot by foot. The men bent forward and sometimes, if the barge happened to give a sheer in a stream, they almost lay on the ground, and waited till she could recover herself.

On the island below the bridge, a rail was elevated on poles to keep the rope clear of the bushes as the men were towing on the bank itself. An iron pulley-wheel was fixed on the wall of the bridge, facing down-stream, to be used by those boats which were going to the quay above the bridge. When the men got upon the bridge, by the stone steps which were provided for the purpose, they passed the rope over this pulley, and proceeded along the bridge towards the town. When the barge came almost to the bridge, the captain had some sharp work. At a shout, each man slipped his breast-band clear of the rope, the tow was hauled in with haste, the mast was lowered and the barge, with plenty of way on her, entered the arch. As her bow appeared above the bridge, a rope was dropped aboard and attached to her, men running with the other end to the causeway on the upper side, keeping up sufficient way to allow her to slant to her berth to be moored. The men then came across in a boat and their particular contract was completed.[2]

Thames halers used similar breast-straps, which are shown in a rare print of Isleworth of about 1775. Mavor, in *The Agriculture of Berkshire* (1809), says the

towing lines, up to 220 yards in length, weighed six to seven hundredweight (a third of a ton), and were frequently useless after three voyages. The strain on rope and men can be envisaged when he says that, at times in the lower district (below Windsor), a barge might be drawn 200 or 300 yards over the gravelly bed of the river. There are interesting estimates from about 1770 of the cost of hauling a barge from London to Reading and from Mapledurham to Oxford in the Oxford Record Office, quoted by Dr Prior in *Fisher Row*.

Illustrations show that the tow-line was invariably attached to the top of the mast, probably via a pulley block. The height was needed to keep the enormous length of the rope clear of the water and obstructions such as osier beds. A near mid-barge towing point was preferable because, if towed from the bow, any craft will invariably be dragged straight into the bank. Some illustrators, probably the more technically correct, show a second line leading from the bows to join up with the masthead line some distance in front of the barge, giving a pulling point somewhat nearer the bows, and halving the strain put on the masthead. This bow line would have been

connected to the windlass bitts and was adjusted to give a high or low pulling point. Although it is not recorded, great skill must have been required by the steersman, with a long cumbersome rudder behind him, to keep the barge on course and not yawing about, putting undue strain on the towing men or horses. It was particularly difficult when carrying high loads; the boy probably then sat on top, calling out directions. When the tilt was up the steersman had to look through a tunnel of canvas to see where he was going!

Some of today's rivermen, recalling the 1950s, say that if the only tug on the Oxford district was miles away, gangs of six men regularly towed 30-ton ballast barges from Oxford to Benson. One present tug-skipper remembers towing a seven ton flat from Shillingford to Benson single-handed.

Strings of horses were already in regular use for

37 Cruise boat *Firebrand*, 1960. Modern halers towing the converted barge along St John's lock cut towards Lechlade. The tow path ends just downstream at 'Bloomers' Hole' and the horse has had to be led on a detour over St John's Bridge

38 Sunbury Lock, 1834. Built in 1812, the lock is no more than a timber braced hole in the ground with gates at either end. The lock keeper's wife may be selling provisions to the crew of the spritsail barge, while patient horses rest before towing upstream. (W. Tombleson)

towing from at least 1600 or so at Hedsor – and presumably on other difficult reaches – but the use of horses was the exception rather than the general rule until well into the eighteenth century. Until then it may have been common to see gangs of ragged men waiting at town wharfs, fighting for a chance to earn a penny towing up the next reach; barefoot, sometimes up to the waist in icy water, bearing on their shoulders a hand-tearing cable which in winter might weigh up to a ton when waterlogged or stiff with ice. Gangs of up to 80 men might be required during flood times, but labour was easy to come by – there were always plenty of landless and destitute peasants, especially at the time of the enclosures. The halers were 'usually [of] the worst possible character and terror to the whole neighbourhood of the river',

probably more out of desperate need than criminal intent.

On the other hand one gets the impression that the bargemen were thought to be a much higher class of person, well paid and conscientious. Illustrious personages like Samuel Pepys found them entertaining company. He describes on 2 June 1668 'Taking into my boat, for company, a man that desired passage; a certain Western bargeman, with whom I had good sport, talking of the old woman of Woolwich and telling him the whole story', and on 14 May, 1669 'so home, sullen, but then my wife and I by water with my brother, as high as Fulham, talking and singing, and playing the rogue with the Western bargemen, about the women of Woolwich, which mads them, and so back home to supper and to bed.' Unfortunately, the story of the women of Woolwich is lost for ever.

BARGEMEN IN COURT
The bargemen were notorious for their highly colourful and inventive language: 'they use singular and even quite extraordinary terms, and generally very

39 Above Marlow 'Ware', *c.* 1810. Lunch is cooking under the tilt as a hay-filled barge is sailed and poled towards the lock. (Artist unknown)

coarse and dirty ones, and I cannot explain them to you', and they could be violent. Pepys would have been well advised to steer clear of a certain William Honnor of Great Marlow, who in 1682 pleaded guilty at the Bucks Quarter Sessions to stealing a saw, a case of knives, five pheasants, and other things from Sir John Borlase. Thereupon it was ordered that the gaoler 'doe, upon Satturday next about the midd time of the day, fasten the said Honnor to the breech of a cart and strippe him naked from waste uppwards and whipp him from the gaole doore to the George signe post in Aylesbury and round the same, and soe to the gaole doore again untill his body bee bloddy, and so to be discharged, payinge his fees.'

Bill Honnor again came before the court three years' later with three other Marlow men, for using guns, nets and 'other engins' to destroy game, and again in 1690 with the Hubbart family, for unlawfully keeping nets for poaching. In 1694 he caused Hugh Lydall, the Marlow constable, considerable trouble for allowing him to escape. In 1702, one would think old enough now to know better, he was

indicted with Thomas Bray for rioting and assaulting John Bedient. In 1708, getting even more cantankerous in his old age, he and also his charming wife are last heard of when indicted for being common night walkers, profane swearers and disturbers of the peace.

Bargemen were not above stealing from their fellows. In 1701 Jeremiah Hollis and Edward Lawrence were prosecuted by Marlow Bargemaster William East for stealing 20 yards of barge cable. Some cheated the more gullible of their earth-bound countrymen, such as in 1712 when two Oxford bargemen, William Rowland and his son, went on a jaunt to remote Winslow, in Bucks, and there defrauded linen draper William Giles and his son, 'using and exercising unlawful games, i.e. cups and balls'.

Despite their obvious shortcomings, the bargemen were a resilient and intrepid breed and, with the wherrymen of the lower river, they were a major

40   Eton College from Windsor, detail, 1793. A truly massive Western barge drifts downstream while the crew sort out the cargo. Correct weight distribution must have been vital. (J. Farington)

source of recruits for the Navy. Many a young lad, after a rollicking night in the riverside pubs around Queenhithe, found himself impressed aboard one of His Majesty's men o'war. Men were not even safe from the press gang inland. In Buckinghamshire in 1708 under an Act of Queen Anne, William Edwards and John Fryer were handed over by the local constables to Captain William Akers's Company in the Honourable Brigadier Hans Hamilton's Regiment 'for the better and speedier manning of Her Majestie's fleet'.

Many men 'jumped ship' and some were recaptured back on their home ground. About 1700, Daniel Holderness (a familiar surname in the Cookham area), a 'Mariner belonging to His Majesties Ship The Sandwich', was ordered to be taken from Marlow to Wycombe Bridewell and detained until the Sherrif came for him.

A sailor's life was hard and uncertain with little pay, no pensions, and, if wounded, no insurance to fall back on. Only occasionally was a small amount given out of county funds if the cripple could produce a certificate to prove he was wounded in action. The certificate that Benjamin Young showed the court stated that 'he served his present Majestie in the late warr against the French by the space of four years in his Majesties ship called the Albermarle' and was wounded. A few years earlier in 1691, Marlow bargeman Ralph Thompson was paid two pounds at the Wendover Sessions by one of the treasurers of the maimed soldiers, upon production of a certificate that he 'was imprest and sett on shipboard the Vanguard in the warrs against the Dutch in the year 1666, and the two fleets being engaged on St James's Day in the same year and there was wounded in the right arme, shoulder, and cheek, and being now very impotent.'[3]

A century-and-a-half later, another bargeman saved himself from going to court by displaying a printed notice outside the little theatre at Henley:

WHEREAS I WILLIAM DICKS OF NEWBURY, bargeman did on Saturday Night last, wantonly throw a Quart Mug, with Beer in it from the Gallery into the Pit of the Theatre, while the Play was performing, which might have materially injured Persons sitting therein, for which offence the Manager had me taken into Custody, and commenced a Prosecution against me, but on my making this public Acknowledgment of my Offence and paying the Expenses already incurred, he has kindly consented to stop all Proceedings; and I hope this will be a caution to all Persons not to behave in the like manner.

William Dicks. Henley, 17 February, 1812.[4]

5 Seventeenth-century disorders

THE HEDSOR CHANNEL

Growing prosperity during Elizabeth's reign had brought trade to the river and barges were increasing in size and numbers. Wharfs expanded, and many of our well-known riverside inns probably developed then, as resting places for the crews, and as a rendezvous between bargemasters and local agents who dealt with orders for goods to and from London and intermediate towns. The inns could also have been used to contract the gangs of halers who towed barges upstream. A few riparian landowners were quick to enter the towing business with horse teams, although there was no obligation, as now, to maintain the haling way or towing path in any particular condition. Because of the expense of upkeep, horses were only rarely used at this time, and where they were the towing rights were jealously guarded. Teams of horses plus a 'carter' were supplied by the landlord or his tenant, and no other forms of towing allowed. The cost of the toll depended on the distance over the property, the size of the barge and therefore the number of horses required.

Some illuminating early-seventeenth-century records associated with horse towing come from Hedsor in Buckinghamshire, where an important wharf had already been in use for centuries. In 1605 the Lord of the Manor, Rowland Hynde, settled the estate on his descendants, including the wharfs and the 'horseing of barges'. At about the same time he was in dispute, not for the first time, with his neighbour Henry Manfield of Taplow, whose house once stood somewhere near the later illustrious Cliveden House.[1] Another smaller wharf lay just downstream from Hedsor on Manfield's land. This was Page's Wharf, tucked beneath the impressive chalk cliff opposite the present Cookham Lock. To help his case, Hynde drew a detailed map of the river channels, and this has been handed down to successive owners of the wharf.

To appreciate the details of the dispute one should know something of the geography of this picturesque area. The river below Cookham bridge divides into four channels, all of which have been altered in name and use over the centuries. The southernmost is the paper mill stream or 'Lollybrook', previously 'Babhams Water'. The next, Odney Weir Stream, was originally 'The Millpond Fishery', the channel for a long-forgotten medieval mill. The third was 'Sashes Stream', which according to Hynde's map once bisected Sashes Island. An easterly portion of this may have been filled in – possibly in the eighteenth century – but the rest was utilized as part of Cookham lock, cut in 1830. Up until that time the northernmost channel, the Hedsor Wharf stream, had always been the main navigation channel.

In the enquiry held at Beaconsfield, Hynde complained that Manfield, apparently at the instigation of bargemen from Henley and members of the local Holderness family, had tried to make his own Sashes Stream navigable by dredging, cutting down trees and demolishing part of the 'Warborow', the ancient man-made weir or bank which extended out into the main river at the head of Sashes Island, and which had probably been built originally to divert the main stream via Hedsor. Hynde was worried that he would be deprived of his towing income and the wharf would be by-passed.

Several witnesses made depositions that the wharf stream was too shallow, because of the chalk stones

41 Cliveden Reach, 1811. A heavy barge with a short
mast is towed downstream towards Maidenhead Bridge.
The channel to the right is rather fanciful, unless there is
local flooding! (W. B. and C. Cooke)

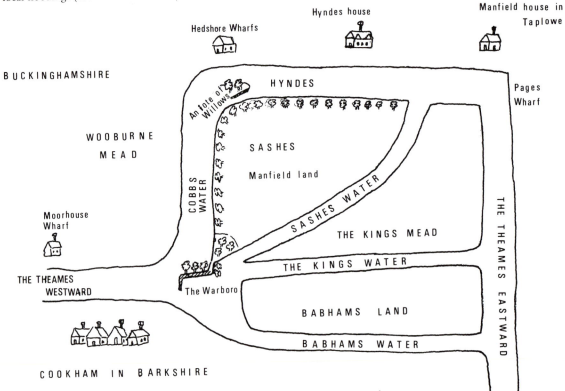

The Thames Channels at Cookham c. 1605[2]

42 Hedsor Wharf, c. 1800. Barges wait to load Chiltern timber. (Artist unknown)

in places on the riverbed (a complaint that was still being made two centuries later). But a witness for Hynde, Hugh Cotterell, a 70-year-old fisherman and former owner of three or four barges at one time, said that the passage was easy. His son Richard confirmed this and said that barges only went aground because that in his time 'ye burthen and bigness of the barges are increased well nigh half'. He stated that Crannoll, the wharfinger, had refused to 'horse up' a Holderness barge via Hedsor because that summer, during a time of high water, Holderness had refused to go that way and went through the Sashes Stream instead 'which was a loss unto the said Crannoll in his barging'. Richard went on to say that there was not sufficient water in Sashes Stream for Western barges and 'did this summer see eight Tilt boats with passengers ly at ground by reason of the shallowness of the water' and even empty Tilt boats could not pass. These light passenger-carrying craft, clinker-built and double-ended like Viking ships, and propelled by sail and oar, were extensively used on the lower Thames, but it is a revelation to

find that they were also apparently common in rural areas. The name comes from the tilt or awning which protected the passengers from the elements.

It seems that river folk were prosperous and healthy and lived to a comparatively ripe old age. Another 70-year-old witness was former bargeman and now labourer, Francis Paget, who with great aplomb agreed that Sashes Brook was so shallow 'As a man might passe over drye in a low paire of shooes'.

Before leaving these Beaconsfield depositions it is worth mentioning that one witness, John Bolt of Taplow, in advocating improvements at Hedsor, mentions that it would make the passage easier for barges to and from Abingdon. So it would seem that at this time bargemen were trading from this affluent town through Sutton flash locks, before the seventeenth-century improvements by the Oxford to Burcot Commissioners, to be discussed later.

Although they undoubtedly enjoyed a good swearing match amongst themselves, bargemen, or at least the Cost-Bearers, or Masters, were not uncouth peasants. Many were highly articulate yeomen with a high standing in the community. John Dodson was one of several generations of Cookham bargemen, and in 1637 was wealthy enough to make

43 Sion House, Isleworth (detail) *c.* 1670. Depicting craft of the upper tideway in Samuel Pepys's day. A splendidly untidy Western barge, the hull apparently sagging under the weight of cargo, is passed by a wherry and a fast tilt boat, driven along by four oarsmen and a small spritsail. A small state barge moves sedately upstream. (Jan Griffier). *By kind permission of His Grace the Duke of Northumberland*

a loan to a relation in London. This was to be repaid at a house on Brooks Wharf, Queenhithe, one of the major wharfs for upper Thames barges. Later bargemen servicing the Cookham and Bourne End area into the nineteenth century, such as the Turners and Wiggintons, also used Brooks Wharf. Another John Dodson made a fortune in tinplate for the Royal Dockyards and in 1716 became High Sheriff for Berkshire.

POUND LOCKS

In 1605 'boates and barges of great content and carriage' were trading regularly up and down the river, from London to within a few miles of Oxford. At Burcot, on the Wittenham loop above Dorchester, the heaviest goods had to be unloaded and transferred to wagons for the last few creaking miles by road to the city. Lighter cargoes may have been transferred to shallower-draughted vessels which could navigate up to Oxford and beyond. There appear to have been few problems for craft trading westwards from Oxford. In 1612, Richard Whistler, the leaseholder of Sutton Courteney Mills, was granted a lease for a wharf by St Helen's Church at Abingdon on condition that he made a lock at Sutton, and the river from there to St Helen's bridge be 'from time to time navigable whereby the Western barges may pass'.[3] The 1585 survey mentions two flash locks already in existence at Sutton; was another needed because these were derelict, or were they just inadequate for the now larger barges? Perhaps the lock stipulated was a pound lock, for a privately-built one was certainly in existence by the 1630s, directly underneath part of the Sutton Mills. It became part of the improvements begun by the Oxford to Burcot Commissioners – but being priva-

Abingdon.

44 St Helen's Wharf and Church, Abingdon, 1847.
Barges lie on a sloping 'hard' at the foot of the
fifteenth-century Long Alley almshouses. To the right
stands the seventeenth-century 'Anchor' public house,
demolished in 1884. Behind are Brick Alley almshouses.
(J. Thorne)

45 Abingdon, 1985. Thames Water Authority tug
Kennett II, built in 1969 by Cunis of Woolwich, tows a
ballast barge passed Brick Alley and Long Alley
almshouses. The steps mark the site of 'The Anchor'

tely owned was notorious for having some of the highest tolls on the river.

The poor condition of the main artery of trade downstream from Oxford was a thorn in the side of the University and merchants of a town which appears to have somewhat recovered from the trials of the previous two centuries or more. In 1607 the so-called Oxford to Burcot Commission was formed by the City and University and the important landowners in the surrounding counties. Apart from ordering a quantity of timber which was to be used for river improvement, but in the end went to Sir Thomas Bodley's library, they did very little, until the River Improvement Act of 1624 forced them into action. No doubt the Act was prompted by the demand from the capital for Cotswold stone from the Oxfordshire quarries, but there was also an increasing demand in Oxford for sea coal and other necessities from London. Another factor was that the carriage of heavy goods by wagon, had made the Oxfordshire roads almost impassable in winter. The 1624 Act authorized the building of three pound locks below Oxford, at Iffley and Sandford Mills and on the Swift Ditch, an ancient channel of the Thames which by-passes Abingdon around Andersey Island.

The flash lock system was wasteful and inconvenient for all concerned. However, long ago some unknown genius had already discovered that craft could be raised and lowered to different levels by floating them into a chamber of water not much longer than the craft themselves. Canals linking navigable rivers were being built in China as far back as 200 BC, using single stop-log gates on the flash lock principle for changes in level. The best known of these is the Grand Canal to Peking which by the thirteenth century was 700 miles (1100k) long. It is likely that here, at an early date, stop-log gates were being placed close together, making the first pound locks. It was not until the fourteenth century that the idea appeared in Europe, when large basins connecting Dutch rivers with canals incorporated two sets of portcullis gates. In the next century, pound locks with portcullis type gates were built by Bertola on several canals leading to Milan, but the credit for the invention of the pound lock incorporating mitre gates with built-in vertical sluices goes to Leonardo da Vinci, who sketched out the design of the lock as we know it today for the San Marco Lock on the Naviglio Interno, Milan, in 1495.[4]

The modern lock consists of a chamber with vertical walls (usually parallel to each other but the shapes have varied over the centuries – there have even been circular basins) with a pair of solid wooden mitre gates at either end. The heel post of each gate is held by a metal strap to the top of the lock wall, and by a socket in a cill on the river bed in which it pivots. As a gate closes it butts up against its partner and at the same time comes up against a cill at the bottom of the river, set in the form of a shallow Vee, the point of the Vee facing upstream. In the same way that a pointed arch can withstand enormous pressures from above, mitre gates can hold back thousands of tons of water pressing against them and not collapse inwards. Yet when the water level is equal on both sides they may be opened with minimal force.

The upper gate cill is set at the depth of the upper section of the river or canal so that there is then a drop down on to the floor of the chamber, the depth of which depends on the height of the 'step' we have to surmount. The tail or downstream cill, and therefore of course the base of the tail gates, will be correspondingly lower. The cills are usually at a depth slightly exceeding the deepest-draughted vessel expected. To fill and empty the chamber, water is let in and out through apertures in the base of the gates by the raising or lowering of sluice gates, or paddles worked by various means. Some locks, especially on the canals, have ground sluices or tunnels in the lock walls, again worked by paddles.

The first pound locks in England were built in 1564–7 for the lateral canal alongside the River Exe, making navigation possible from Exeter to the sea. These locks had mitre gates at the head and a single gate at the tail. A few years later (1571–4), the River Lee was improved at Waltham Abbey, with the help of a pound lock with two sets of mitre gates. The first Thames 'turnpikes', as they were then called, at Iffley, Sandford and Swift Ditch, were open for business by 1635. The original structures appear to have been built with timber walls which soon deteriorated, for in 1651 the wall of Swift Ditch collapsed and free-stone was brought from Kennington to build a stronger lock. Iffley and Sandford were also rebuilt in stone, probably on several occasions through the centuries, and their remains may be seen alongside their modern counterparts.

46 Iffley Mill and Lock, 1866. The site of one of the first pound locks on the Thames

47 Culham Bridge, over the Swift Ditch, near Abingdon, 1985. The fifteenth-century bridge may have been widened to provide this navigation arch for the Oxford to Burcot improvements, which included the temporary re-use of this ancient channel for barge traffic. The masonry shows wear possibly caused by towlines two centuries ago

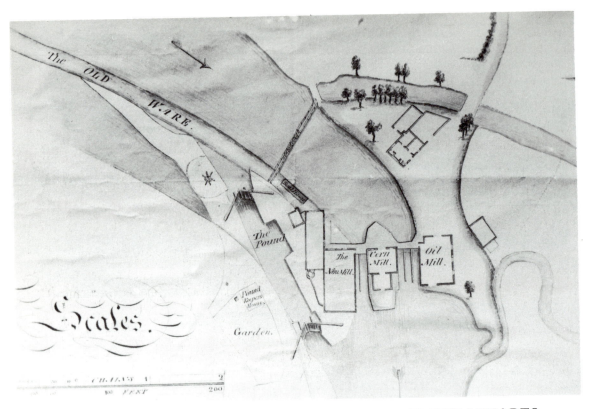

48 Marlow Mills estate plan, 1816. The first poundlock of 1770. Apparently after over 40 years the 'old ware' had not been completely dredged away. The capstan above the lock was probably required to haul barges up past the mill races

Swift Ditch Lock has a different history because the navigation channel later reverted to the old Abingdon stream when the eighteenth-century series of locks were built.

To see the tiny Swift Ditch today it is difficult to visualize that huge barges once passed along its winding course, but that they did is proved by the gateless masonry walls of the old lock, which for over 300 years have stood in their leafy setting at the upper end of the stream. This old lock may never have been a great success, because of the silting up of the channel below it. Each time a lock is filled and emptied a certain amount of silt and gravel is drawn through, which tends to build up a shoal below the lock. The lesson was learnt by the engineers because later locks were sited at the lower end of lock cuts, so that debris was discharged into the main river, where there is less chance of shoaling.

TRADE UNDER THE STUARTS

At the same time that the first Thames locks were under construction a certain John Taylor took a trip on the river. Taylor (1580–1653) was a well known Thames wherryman, poet, pamphleteer and traveller, much concerned with river improvements. His description in *Thame Isis* of 1632 includes:

... Then Marlow Lock is worse, I must confess
the water is so pinched with shallowness.
Beneath which is a weare should be defaced
and Cottrells weare of Cookham be displaced
A weare to one Holdernesse belong
Which doth the river most injourious wrong
Near which a spring runs from the chalkie hills
Which not long ago did turn two mills.
A stop against Taplow Warren doth much spread
Next Bolters Lock, (a mile from Maidenhead).

Five years later he supplied another valuable description of river trade in his *Carriers Cosmographie* '... To Bull Wharfe (near Queenhithe) there doe come and go great boats twice or thrice every week betwixt London and Kingston ... great boats that doe carry passengers and goods betwixt London and Maydenhead ... doe come every Munday and

49 Romney Lock, *c.* 1865. The original structure of 1797 just before the rebuilding in 1869. Many early pound locks were constructed entirely of timber

Thursday and goe away upon Tuesdays and Thursdays. The Reading boat is to be had at Queenhithe weekly.'[5]

A certain amount of barge traffic continued throughout the Civil War, despite the obstructions of demolished bridges and locks. The Royalists controlled much of the river in the early days, provisions and munitions getting through to the garrisons at Reading and Oxford. The voyages must have been fraught with danger from attack by Parliamentary skirmishers. For instance, in March 1645 'some great boats' were sunk while taking supplies from Newbridge to Oxford.[6] A bargeman's lot could not have been a happy one at the time. Even less happy was the lot of four barge loads of Scots prisoners, who in 1648 were taken down river from an overcrowded Windsor Castle to Gravesend to await transportation.[7]

The bargeman's life was not made much easier in 1650, when an act of the Puritan Parliament forbade the movement of all river traffic on Sundays. Troops stationed along the rivers enforced the ban. One can imagine the chagrin of a bargemaster with a perishable cargo having to lose 24 hours travelling time and perhaps a good flush of water into the bargain, and having to lie aground for several days. The Commonwealth Acts fell with the Restoration but the Sunday ban was re-enacted and not repealed until 1827, though not strictly enforced – although in about 1710 Thomas Cocke of Fifield in Berkshire was arrested by the Hambleden Constable for the offence and was indicted and fined 6s 8d after escaping from custody.

The second half of the seventeenth century brings many references to Western barges going from London to Oxford almost daily, with provisions of all kinds, and returning with West Country and Chiltern timber for the building of merchant and fighting ships. From all the riverside towns came vast quantities of that very important commodity, malt.

After the Great Fire in 1666 Cotswold stone went down to help in the rebuilding of London, including

50 Folly Bridge Wharf, Oxford, 1970. The early-nineteenth-century warehouse and a crane are reminders of centuries of barge trade between London and Oxford

Wren's churches and St Paul's Cathedral. Much good quality stone came from high up in the Windrush valley from Master Mason Christopher Kempster's quarries at Taynton, near Burford, from where it was carted ten miles south to the wharf on the stripling Thames beside the beautiful medieval bridge at Radcot. Arkel in *Oxford Stone* quotes entries from Kempster's Day Book which include:

Sept. 21, 1672. Then was loaded into Humphrey Duffins boat 75 ffoot of ston at Ratcat.
Sept. 26, 1672. Then was loaded into Houses boat 9 tunn two ffoot ffrom ratcat pd. him then fivety shillings, 2. 1od.

In the Oxford to Burcot Commissioners' Account and Minute Book dating from 1650 (Oxfordshire Record Office), the Howes family are mentioned as owning barges in Oxford and the Duffins at Abingdon, where they also rented the early Swift Ditch Lock.

Passenger traffic on the lower river was in its heyday, and there were said to be 10,000 small boats between the Fleet River and Windsor. Wherries were rowed by members of that tough company of watermen at least as far as Maidenhead. The sleek wherry was a far more comfortable and cheaper means of transport than the first cumbersome coaches now appearing on 'those bad ways'.

In the late seventeenth century the state of the river for barge traffic was, as always, giving cause for concern. One of the campaigners for improvement was Andrew Yarranton. In 1677 he enthused over the idea of linking the Severn with the Thames, first thought of ten years before, and gave his reasons for an inland route to the west coast.

Of necessity, we must always be sailing round about the Island, carrying and recarrying such heavy commodities from port to port to be taken into the more inward parts of the Kingdom, otherwise the charge of carrying such goods by land would rise to a very vast charge, the highways of our island being very uneven, and the ways therein in wintertime very bad.

The proposal was also aired in a pamphlet four years later in *A dialogue betwixt Sam, the Datchet Ferryman and Tom an Oxford Bargeman, upon the Kings calling a Parliament at Oxford*, quoted by Tighe and Davis in *The Annals of Windsor*. The tract also tells us of the rivalry which existed between London and Oxford, and anticipates William Cobbett's later complaint that London, 'The Great Wen' (wart), was draining the countryside of its wealth.

TOM: They say the King will make us a way Westward to Bristol, for our barges, and has sent for Dutchmen that can make boats go by land as well as by water, and then Bristol will be London. The saucy rogues, the other day at Queenhithe, were ready to brain us, and threatened to fire the barges, because we belonged to Oxford. If the King would take my counsel, he should come no more amongst them, for one seven years; I would make the proud rogues know themselves better.

SAM: I am not for that, Tom, neither, for that would quite spoil our ferry, when all is done London is London.

TOM: And will be London, that is, a nest of unthankful rogues, that hate us country gentlemen, though they get all they have by us. What would London be worth, if it were not for the country? And faith, since all of the wealth of the country is gotten thither, by the King's living so long amongst them, I hope his Majesty will even now live in the country, till their money be brought into the country again.

SAM: I could agree well enough to all thou sayest, but only for this ferry, and that would be quite ruined, if the King should leave London.

TOM: For that, if the Dutchmen come, they will dig so many cuts to make the Thames run from our town to Bristol, I warrant thee. Then mayest get a new ferry, and better than this, upon some of those new cuts . . .

Land carriage from London to Oxford at the time was about £3 per ton, three times more than by water, and the cost could be very much greater when pack-horses had to carry bulk goods, such as coal or salt. Timber had to be left at the forest edge at the onset of winter rains, and no attempt was made to haul it to where it was required until dry weather returned – maybe six months later. There were of course delays on the river also, but usually only of one or two weeks duration, although Yarranton states they could last six weeks. Barges were still being held up by the contrariness of the millers and flash lock owners, especially during low water conditions, and exorbitant tolls were being charged. Complaints throughout the years led to the Act of 1695, when a new commission from riparian counties was formed, and tolls and flash times fixed for a nine year period.[8]

6 Eighteenth-century trade

SUNKEN MALT

In the eighteenth century, Berkshire and adjacent counties were rich barley growing areas and malting was one of the main industries of upper Thames towns. Although much malt was needed locally, beer then being the staple drink of the country people, the greater bulk of it was shipped down the Thames to the London brewers. The Bucks Sessions Records of the time give many details of river traffic, and in particular the carriage of malt. Before a local maltster could send his produce to the London markets the load was weighed and checked by the local excise officer, and a duty paid. If by any chance the barge was sunk and the malt lost, then the duty could be reclaimed through the courts. For instance, in 1705 the *Kings Arms* of Henley went down near Boveney and duty on 120 quarters was returned to five different maltsters. (Defoe reckons there are about ten quarters to the ton). The following year *The Ship of Henley* also went down at Boveney, with the loss of 134 quarters, and in the same year *Little Dove* of Oxford, at Harleyford House above Marlow, with 165 quarters.

In 1711 *The Angell* of Henley (a name for all thirsty boatmen to conjure with) sank at Marlow, and 16 Henley maltsters lost 340 quarters, collectively receiving a rebate of over £80. A certain widow, Elizabeth Tovey, alone received £12 for 60 quarters. In 1713, the *Unicorn* of 90 tons burden left Hedsor wharf with a cargo which included 32 quarters belonging to Beaconsfield maltster, Francis Carter. Only two miles downstream the laden barge went out of control at the great flash lock at Boulters, leaving another unhappy maltster up on the hill. Three years later *The Rose and Crown* was

another Henley barge to go down at Marlow, laden with 410 quarters for London. Twelve Henley maltsters, including Samson and Caleb, of that devout Tovey family, received the bad news and their refunds.

In 1723 William Davenport of West Wycombe and Thomas Darling of Great Marlow claimed that 57 quarters of malt, on which they paid duty of £11 8s, had been sunk. It was afterwards salvaged and mixed with other malt, presumably after most of the surplus river water had been squeezed out. The two gentlemen received an allowance of £3 3s as the local inspector reported that only part of the malt had been completely lost. In 1728 the total amount of duty on 105 quarters of malt was refunded to Thomas Olyffe, Chiltern maltster, when the barge *Mealcock*, owned by Ralph Rose of Little Marlow, went down near Boulters flash lock loaded with malt and paper. In the years 1732–9 Olyffe was sending 1500 quarters to London annually. Most of the foregoing claims were made at the Easter Sessions, which leads one to believe that bargemasters were attempting to navigate during dangerous early spring flood conditions and paid the penalty. With little or no insurance in those days, that penalty was high. However, most cargoes got through reasonably intact, including in 1711 the Wycombe Parish church bells via Spade Oak wharf to London, for recasting; and presumably back again the same way.

RIVERSIDE WHARFS

An old brick farmhouse which may have once been part of Spake Oak wharf still stands on the river bank just above the sailing club at Bourne End. The

51 A southwest Prospect of London, *c. 1750*. Far from the rural upper Thames, two Western barges fight their way back up past fishing boats, wherries and lighters, after delivering their malt to the City. Queenhithe lies among the jumble of wharfs to the right of St Paul's. (Print published by Bowles)

52 Below Henley Bridge, *c. 1900*. For centuries a large percentage of the town's population were involved in the malt trade. In the twentieth century barges such as these were still used to carry cereals to and from local mills

towpath from Cookham crossed the river at this point and continued to Marlow on the Buckinghamshire shore. At one time this was an important stopping place for river traffic, and in the Middle Ages the abbess of the nearby nunnery of Little Marlow undoubtedly exacted a toll from bargemen towing through the estate which ran down to the riverside. The nuns would have run a wharf on a commercial basis, receiving goods from London and exporting timber and country produce collected from the surrounding parishes.

After the Dissolution the wharf continued to prosper and by the end of the seventeenth century was shipping out large quantities of malt. The wharfinger then was Ralph Rose, who was born in 1664 and who by 1701, either by inheritance or business acumen, was rich enough to build himself a magnificent brick house in the nearby hamlet of Well End, where it stands to this day proudly bearing a terracotta plaque with the initials 'R.R. 1701' high up on an external wall. Ralph is men-

tioned in the Buckinghamshire Quarter Sessions Records in 1724 as wharfinger at Little Marlow. Spade Oak wharf and the nearby site of the old nunnery are of course within the old parish boundary of Little Marlow, but some way from the village, which was sited away from the river on slightly higher ground. Old Ralph lived to the ripe old age of 87. He died in 1751, and was buried in Little Marlow churchyard where his grave may be seen today. The Rose family continued to live in Well End. The name of Ralph Rose occurs in *Kelly's Directories* in 1847 and 1877, and the Misses Rose still lived in the mellowed brick house into this century.

An estate map of 1762 shows two other nearby wharfs in Wooburn Parish, Lanes's, at the site of the present Bourne End boatyard, and Robinson's, near the confluence of the little River Wye. They served a multitude of papermakers, maltsters and millers of a highly industrious Wycombe Valley. In evidence at an 1846 House of Commons committee inquiry for a proposed railway line to High Wycombe, paper maker Charles Venables stated that at one time there were 19 paper mills and 11 corn mills on the Wye. Between one and two hundred sacks of flour once went weekly to London via the Thames. Now there

53   A view of Eton (detail), 1793. A timber wharf below Windsor Bridge. (J. Farington)

were about 5000 tons of coal and something like 4000 tons of rags and old rope annually brought upstream for the paper makers. Finished paper and board went back to London from the wharfs.

The usual idea of a wharf is a stone or timber quay with vertical sides against which vessels can moor to be unloaded. Prints show this type at Maidenhead bridge in the eighteenth century and Oxford and Windsor bridges in the nineteenth. At the latter there was a large swinging derrick crane controlled with ropes from either end of the quay. However, this kind of wharf appears to be the exception rather than the rule. Generally, wharf areas consisted of a sloping gravel hard, natural or man-made, on which flat-bottomed barges would ground, often bows on, and cargoes transferred to and from shore by gang-plank. Important wharfs at Hedsor and Abingdon functioned in this way.

READING AND NEWBURY

The importance of river traffic in the eighteenth century must not be underestimated. It has been said that at one time up to 95 per cent of goods to and from Reading were carried by water. Daniel Defoe gives a graphic account of the town in *A Tour Through England and Wales* published in 1724.

A very large and wealthy town, handsomely built, the inhabitants rich and driving a very great trade. The town lies on the River Kennet, but so near the Thames, that the largest barges which they use, may come up to the town bridge, and there they have wharfs to load, and unload them. Their chief trade is by this water navigation to and from London, though they have necessarily a great trade into the country, for the consumption of the goods which they bring by their barges from London, and particularly coals, salt, grocery wares, tobacco, oyls, and all heavy goods.

They send from hence to London by these barges very great quantities of malt and meal, and these are the two principle articles of their loadings, of which, so large are those barges, that some of them, as I was told, bring a thousand, or twelve hundred quarters of malt at a time, which, according to the ordinary computation of tonnage in the freight of other vessels, is from a hundred, to a

54 Cookham, 1811. A barge with rounded bow, probably from the Kennet or Thames and Severn Canal, with the awning tied up snugly for the night. (W. B. and C. Cooke)

hundred and twenty ton, dead weight.

They also send very great quantities of timber from Reading; for Berkshire being a very well wooded county, and the River Thames a convenient conveyance for the timber. They send most of it, and especially the largest and fairest of the timber, to London, which is generally bought by the shipwrights in the river, for the building of merchant ships; as also, the like trade of timber is at Henley, another town on the Thames, and at Maidenhead. . . .

In 1723 one year before the publication of Mr Defoe's *Tour* in which he extolled the wonders of Reading, the Kennet Navigation Company flattened the remains of the old castle at Newbury and proceeded to dig a huge basin and wharf capable of dealing with ten 100 ton barges at a time. The Act

55   Datchet Bridge, 1834. Possibly a Kennet size barge with a budgett stern and wooden cabin, although it is difficult to see where cabin ends and cargo begins! (W. Tombleson)

for 'The clearing of a passage for boats, lighters etc., upon the Kennet from the wharf or present common landing place at Reading to Newbury' was passed in 1714, but the work of building 11 miles of new cuts and 20 locks was not begun until 1719.

From the beginning the work was fraught with hazards, the greatest of which was the opposition of the Mayor, the Corporation and practically every man, woman and child of Reading. Up to that time Reading had the monopoly of trade over a vast area to the south and west. Much of this would now be lost to their lesser neighbour 16 miles away, so until the final completion of the scheme and the stabilization of management and tolls in 1730, the people of Reading did everything in their power to interfere with the construction work and tried to stop all early traffic. On several recorded occasions mobs of 300 or more, led by the Mayor, marched out to do battle with the engineers, breaking down new locks and sinking barges. Loaded barges were laid aground when the water was deliberately run off by sluice

gates being left open, and when they finally reached Reading the crews had to run the gauntlet of the stone-throwing mob. Despite all the opposition, Newbury became one of the busiest inland ports in the south. Country produce such as cheese, meal and malt went to the Company's Downs Wharf, Queenhithe, and the barges returned with coal, iron, deals and groceries. In company with other improved rivers and early canals, the Kennet set an example which led to the canal mania of the new Industrial Age.

THE THAMES COMMISSIONERS

During the eighteenth century, Thames-side towns grew in importance as an increasing amount of country produce was sent to feed the growing population of London. Thousands of tons of cheese and other goods were delivered annually. In return, London was sending up sea-coal to the amount of 80,000 tons a year. Many of the 300 or more barges now trading carried loads well in excess of one hundred tons and when the stream ran fast between 30 and 60 men or a dozen horses might be required to haul them against the current. Thacker quotes a timetable of 1746 by Roger Griffiths, a City bailiff, who lists barge departures from London for many local riverside towns including Guildford on the River Wey, two or three times every week, and also 'to Abindon, Newbery and Reading from the Bull by Brooks Wharf, Queenhithe' every week, also a regular service to Oxfordshire. Flash-lock and bridge tolls could amount to £14 for 60 tons from London to Lechlade. It is interesting to see that craft of this capacity could apparently negotiate the acute bends and shallow reaches for miles above Oxford without much recorded difficulty.

In the mid eighteenth century the country began to stir out of its slow agrarian existence, and country gentlemen decided that there was money to be made from the new mines and machinery, and in the mass-production of cheap goods to meet the needs of a growing population at home and abroad. The enclosures began to drive many landless peasants into the crowded suburbs of the manufacturing towns – where they were eager to subserviate themselves to the mill owners, so that they and their families could live. Moreover, the gentry rushed to join the fashionable game of exploitation of the newly found resources. Many Acts of Parliament at this time centred on the attempts to improve transport facilities for the carriage of bulk raw materials and manufactured goods. The death penalty was imposed for stealing from barges and wharfs, and on deliberate destruction of locks and weirs. The death sentence was also imposed on rioters who damaged the bridges and gates of the new turnpike roads, roads which might take a coach from London to Bath in two days, but which certainly couldn't cope with the many heavy stage wagons – on which were imposed heavy restrictions on weight and wheel size.

In 1729 came the first Thames Commissioners Act, which was meant to obtain some control over the operation of flash locks and the tolls charged 'for the use of all towing paths, either by men or horses, as they are now used'. The Act of 1751 appointed a new body to improve conditions on the Thames above Staines. Over 500 commissioners from the riverside towns, the University of Oxford, and gentry with certain property qualifications were appointed. Apart from annoying the bargemen with an unrealistic draught restriction of three feet (90cm) which was soon changed to four feet (120cm), and a temporary adjustment of tolls, things went on as they always had.

By 1767 barges had reached the incredible load capacity of 200 tons. Flash lock owners blamed their increased tolls on the increase in the size of the vessels, which in turn necessitated an increase in the heights of the weirs, to give greater depth of water.

In 1770 the Commissioners were reinforced by the addition of hundreds of minor landowners and town and parish officials, and were soon to be jolted out of their complacency by several workable schemes for canals from Reading to London, by-passing the Thames altogether. James Brindley was commissioned by the City of London to survey the river between Maidenhead and London, and to suggest improvements. He reported that 12 pound locks should be built (they were, about 40 years later) but proposed that a better economic proposition would be to build a canal from Sonning to Isleworth, crossing the Thames at Monkey Island, Bray. The idea was enthusiastically received by Reading and the City but the Bill was voted out by Parliament, owing to the opposition of the conveniently enlarged Thames Commission, which now included in its ranks most of the M.P.s residing in the valley. Several other similar canals, including one up the

Wye Valley to High Wycombe, were proposed in later years but met the same fate.

The canal schemes did, however, frighten the Commissioners into getting on with the job of improving the river in their jurisdiction, and within three years turf-sided 'turnpikes', as they were first called – said to have been designed by Humphrey Gainsborough, brother of the painter – were built on the middle river at Boulters (on the Taplow Mill Stream), Marlow, Temple, Hurley, Hambleden, Marsh, Shiplake and Sonning. In fact, in all the positions between Reading and Maidenhead in which locks exist today, except for Cookham, which came 60 years later. Many other locks were soon to be built above Reading, after pressure from the committees of the Thames and Severn Canal and the Oxford Canal, which opened in 1789 and 1790 respectively.

In 1774 Bowles's *Draught of the Thames* gave a

total figure of £13 5s in a table of tolls from London to Lechlade, including 7s 6d for the lock at Boulters, 4 shillings for Marlow turnpike, lock, bridge and winch and 3 shillings for Temple Mills lock and turnpike. In 1791 a 60 ton barge paid over £26 in tolls between Lechlade and London – almost double that of 17 years before. This was partly due to charges at the new pound locks (soon to decrease after yet more pressure from the canals) but as can be seen above, also because tolls were still being claimed by the old flash locks which the commissioners were only just beginning to buy up. Freight charges were now about £1 per ton downstream and £1 5s upstream between London and Lechlade, and soon the Thames and Severn Canal Company could offer rates of £1 6s per ton for bulk cargoes all the way to Bristol.

A new Act in 1795 was supposed to reinforce the existing powers of the Commissioners and at the same time recommended that two pound locks should be erected in the Windsor area, at Cuckoo Weir below Boveney and at Romney Island, to help the navigation below Boulters. Permission had to be sought from the City of London in case obstructions

56   Boulters Lock, Maidenhead, *c.* 1870. Built in 1830 as 'Ray Mill Pound', it replaced the 1770 lock on Taplow Mill stream. With the rise of Victorian pleasure boating it became the most famous lock on the river

such as these were likely to interfere with navigation below Staines. Of the two proposed, only Romney was built. The Act also gave powers to widen and consolidate the old haling ways for the use of horses.

At this time negotiations were also taking place between the Commissioners and Frederick, Lord Boston, riparian owner of the dangerous Hedsor bend just below Cookham Ferry, where strong currents and rocky shallows had accounted for the sinking of a number of barges. It was considered to be one of the worst hazards between Reading and Boulters and Lord Boston was asked to clear the shoals and generally improve things, but made no effort to do so. Hedsor was eventually bypassed by Cookham cut and lock in 1830.

Towards the turn of the century the increasing canal trade boosted annual Thames tonnage through Staines towards the 85,000 mark; 70,000 tons was passing through Boulters. The scene on the lower river was that as described by an observer at Brent-

ford '. . . vast numbers of barges coming up the river; they had wind and tide but they had all men to draw them up. I saw 34 men to draw up one but there was several more tied to him.' Canals now brought many products direct from the Midlands and West Country to the Thames valley, where in Reading groceries were as cheap as in London.

During the eighteenth century the greater part of the populations of riverside towns such as Henley and Marlow were said to be made up of bargemen, wharfingers and others connected with the river. They were a force to be reckoned with. After the disastrous summer of 1766, there were many riots over the price of food. At Marlow, it is said that bargemen took over the town and robbed the wealthier citizens – but instead of helping their starving women and children they went on a pub crawl to Maidenhead. Bargemen were again in trouble soon after the opening of the first Boulters Pound Lock on the Taplow millstream in 1772. They found this a nice sheltered backwater in which to lay up, and proceeded to use the grounds of Taplow Court as a thoroughfare into Maidenhead. It was alleged that they made such a nuisance of themselves

57 Hurley, 1834. A heavily-laden barge is towed downstream past the flash lock into the pound lock channel. (W. Tombleson)

58 Hambleden, near Henley, 1974. A typical example of an ancient Thames mill site, showing the long overfall dam or lasher, with the modern flood gates on the site of the flash lock. The old flour mill is on the right and the modern pound lock and cut to the left

that a clause was inserted in the Act of 1774:

And whereas many trespasses have been committed in the Gardens and Plantations of Morough O'Brien Esquire of Taplow Court, by persons belonging to boates, barges, vessels, or floats, which anchor, moor, fasten, or lie, in Taplow millstream . . . It shall not be lawful to anchor, moor, fasten, or lie . . . in any part of Taplow millstream between the lock in the said millstream and a meadow called Clemarsh Meadow.

The master of any vessel breaking the law could be fined up to £5. This law still stands, although it might be difficult to enforce today, as a prosecutor might have to prove the position of the old lock, traces of which have long since vanished. Meanwhile, the normal laws of trespass still apply, and boats negotiating Taplow millstream are advised to keep moving.

7 The connecting navigations

THE THAMES AND SEVERN CANAL

The Thames and Severn Canal was opened in November 1789, and the first barge which passed through the Lechlade was greeted by celebrating crowds and the sound of cannon fire from Edward Loveden's Buscot Park estate. Loveden was a leading Berkshire agriculturalist, a Thames Commissioner, and a champion of canals and such improvements. His interests were purely commercial, and soon Welsh coal was being landed at his wharf at half of the previous cost of north country coal brought up river from London. He charged some of the highest lock tolls at Buscot, which was one of a number of new pound locks urged on the Thames Commissioners by the canal company, to deepen the river between Lechlade and Oxford. However, because the river, like all others, was subject to so many flow variations from drought to flood, the Commissioners were never able or willing to improve the navigation to the satisfaction of the canal proprietors, and it is amazing that for many years the river between Oxford and Lechlade and the canal, which also often suffered from lack of water, were able to cope with deeply-laden barges carrying up to 70 tons. It is unlikely that this tonnage could be carried easily on the upper river today.

The Thames and Severn Canal cut across the Cotswolds from Inglesham on the Thames just west of Lechlade, via the Sapperton Tunnel and the Golden Valley, to join with the Stroudwater Navigation which entered the Severn at Framilode. In the eighteenth century about 400 flat-bottomed sailing craft were trading on the difficult and often dangerous River Severn, about a quarter of them based at the thriving West Country port of Bristol. The larger vessels, which were called trows (rhyming with crow), carried cargoes of up to around one hundred tons, some navigating as far up as Shrewsbury, more than 160 miles from the sea.[1] The trows at this time mainly had the ancient form of square-rigged sail, and were often towed and shoved in the upper reaches. Smaller vessels on the Severn, apparently called frigates or barges, but on the connecting waterways often confusingly also called trows, navigated the highest reaches and the tributaries such as the Warwickshire Avon, some types eventually going through the Thames and Severn Canal on to the Thames.[2]

For centuries the Severn had been a vital highway for the carriage of merchandise between the West Midlands, Gloucester and Bristol. The industrial revolution and the building of the connecting canals such as the Staffordshire and Worcestershire, and later the Worcester and Birmingham, brought many heavy cargoes on to the river, including an ever increasing amount of coal, and it was mainly this trade which the Thames and Severn Canal at first catered for. In 1794 over 16,000 tons were transshipped from Severn trows at the inland port of Brimscombe, where the Stroudwater Canal joined the Thames and Severn. In the nineteenth century the canal company built improved trows for the carriage of coal from Wales and the Forest of Dean, the latter trade reaching a total of 36,000 tons in 1825. However, little of this coal reached as far east as Oxford, where there was overwhelming competition from coal brought down the narrow Oxford Canal, which has outlived its wider competitor. Thames and Severn coal was mainly unloaded at Lechlade, Radcot and Newbridge, while Oxford

Canal coal went westwards as far as Eynsham wharf.

On their way back westwards, Thames and Severn barges carried country produce such as grain and wool from the Cotswolds, but much of the expected trade did not materialize. Attempts were made to promote the much-hoped-for through traffic between Severn ports and the lower Thames, and for a time there was a weekly service from Brimscombe to Hambro Wharf in London. Barges took nine to 10 days on the easterly voyage and 12 to 14 days back. Unfortunately, costs were found to be too high, as there were few cargoes to be found for the return trip, crews still had to be paid and Thames tolls were charged even on empty barges. Even so, although private barge owners were practically non-existent, in the early 1800s the canal company had over 30 barges for the Thames trade. Until 1790 the width of traditional upper Thames barges had been restricted to 11ft 9in (3.58m) by Godstow Bridge,

but they could be up to 88ft (26m) long, giving a very large overall hull area, which meant they could carry 70 tons and draw no more than four feet (120cm) of water. The canal, with locks 90ft (27.5m) long by 12ft (3.65m) wide, was built to handle the largest of these, but they could not proceed west of Brimscombe Port, because of their length; the older Stroudwater Company locks could cope with craft about 15ft (4.6m) wide, but only 65ft (19.5m) long. On the other hand, the smaller of the traditional Severn vessels that could go through the Stroudwater could not proceed east of Brimscombe because they were too wide, and until the company built barges specifically for the Droitwich salt trade and modified trows for the through passage, all cargoes were transhipped at Brimscombe.

The canal did bring advantages to many, and even brought the industrial revolution into the heart of the Thames Valley, for in 1790 Thomas Williams could rebuild and expand the famous Temple Copper Mills near Marlow because of the canal. Smelted copper was brought from Swansea by Severn trow to Brimscombe and transferred to Thames barges for the rest of the voyage through England. The copper

59 Inglesham Round House, *c.* 1900, at the confluence of the Thames and Severn Canal and the Thames near Lechlade. The round lock houses were a unique feature of the canal

sheets produced at Temple continued the journey downstream to the London dockyards, to sheath the hulls of the fighting ships of the Royal Navy.[3]

The Thames and Severn was soon to lose its Bristol to London trade to the Kennet and Avon wide canal, which opened in 1810. The Wilts and Berks Canal which ran through those counties from Semington on the Kennet and Avon to Abingdon-on-Thames, opened the same year. This was a narrow canal, designed for the familiar midlands type of narrowboat, 70ft (21.5m) long and 6ft 10in (2.1m) wide, carrying 20 to 30 tons. A decade later the Wilts and Berks was connected to the Thames and Severn at Latton near Cricklade by the North Wilts narrow canal, which made it possible for waterborn goods in narrowboats to by-pass the difficult upper Thames navigation. Humphrey Household states that in 1839, 1526 narrowboats passed over the summit level of the Thames and Severn; 317 'trows' were also recorded but no Thames barges. The term trow in this case probably refers to barges built locally for the company's Thames trade in traditional Severn or Stroudwater styles, which together with Kennet and Avon forms,

seem to have had some influence on Thames barge design.

THE KENNET AND AVON CANAL

Many of the larger Western barges had by 1809 been superceded by the 128 ton Newbury barges, 109ft (33m) long by 17ft (5.2m) wide, that were built for the Kennet Navigation, which earlier had been much improved by Superintendent Benjamin Barnard. In 1812 there were 22 Thames registered barges with Newbury owners. Fred Thacker in *Kennet Country* gives the names of Parsons, with 11 vessels, Horner 3, Slockock 2, Batten 1, Slockock and Batten (sharing) 2, Quarryington 1, Page 1, King 1.[4] Strangely, Barnard isn't mentioned, although the name occurred often in contemporary local newspapers only a few years earlier. According to research by Mr Tony Ellis on the Kennet barge builders and owners, White and Barnard were operating until 1805 when, on the death of Mr White, it

60 Buscot Lock, *c.* 1883. Built in 1790 as part of the upper river improvements for the Thames and Severn Canal

was announced that Joseph and George Barnard had entered upon a new partnership. These may have been the sons of Superintendent Benjamin Barnard.

The discovery by a metal detector user in 1973, on the riverside at Cookham, of a very large iron forked set-pole shoe brought the name of Barnard physically into the twentieth century. The shoe was about 30ins (75cm) in length, and the weight was guessed at about 20lbs (9 kl), necessary to sink a very buoyant wooden pole to the river bed. It was inscribed with the lettering 'J. and G.B.' (Joseph and George Barnard?), 'Barnard and Sons', and 'Bett and Dewe, Newb.' (the makers?). It is now in Reading Museum, joining many hundreds of other artifacts recovered from the river.

The Kennet and Avon Canal, completed in 1810, linked the Bristol Avon at Bath with the Kennet Navigation at Newbury. The locks were 80ft (24.5m) long and 14ft (4.25m) wide, capable of handling craft carrying up to 60 tons. Within a decade, 70 of these barges were bringing Somerset and Welsh coal, Baltic timber, building stone and groceries to wharfs such as Devizes, Newbury and Aldermaston. But the canal's greatest advantage over the Thames and Severn was that it was a shorter and much more reliable inland route direct from the Port of Bristol to London. Apart from West Country coal and stone, barges carried eastwards Welsh iron, tinplate, copper, timber, grain, flour and Irish provisions. By 1818 over 200 craft were using the Navigation. A voyage from Bristol to London probably took about seven days; an extra day may have been needed for the return trip against a strong current on the Thames.

The canal barges, with maximum dimensions of about 68ft (21m) long by 13ft 9in (4.2m), plus many 70ft narrow boats, soon ousted the earlier 109ft Newbury barges from the Kennet, and in 1834 the

61 A view of Oxford from Godstow, 1822. The lock was built in 1790 as part of the improvement of the upper Thames. (W. Westall)

62 Hambleden, *c.* 1880. *Millers Maid* of Hambleden
Mill. The high transom stern is typical of barges built by
Robbins of Honey Street

63 The 'Barnard' set pole shoe with a standard punt
pole shoe for comparison

64 Kintbury Wharf, Kennet Navigation, *c.* 1910. Corn merchants and millers H. Dolton and Son loading wide boat *Betty* with local grain for shipment to their warehouse at Newbury

owner of the last three of these craft was compensated as the Kennet locks had been reduced in size to save time and water. The 1830s were the peak years for the canal, when the total annual freight carried exceeded 300,000 tons, over three times the Thames and Severn Canal trade.

THE RIVER WEY AND BASINGSTOKE CANAL

The River Wey Navigation, which enters the Thames at Weybridge, is in some respects similar to the Kennet. The river was made navigable for the 15 miles to Guildford by means of artificial cuts and pound-locks as early as 1653, and extended to Godalming in 1763. Its trade was mainly in the agricultural products from Hampshire, Sussex and Surrey for the London markets, and timber for ship building. An inland waterway from London to the south coast was realized in 1816 with the opening of the Wey and Arun Canal, and a further canal, the Portsmouth and Arundel, joined the River Arun to

Portsmouth in 1822. In common with many canals these monumental works of surveying and engineering were never a financial success; the Portsmouth and Arundel Canal only lasted 25 years and the Wey and Arun 55.

The $37\frac{1}{2}$ mile Basingstoke Canal which was opened in 1794 was comparatively successful and managed to stay open until 1946. It runs in an east-west direction and joins the Wey at Byfleet, therefore using only three miles of that navigation to reach the Thames. In its first few years it boosted the annual trade on the Wey from about 33,000 tons to 54,000 tons. The peak was reached in 1838 with nearly 90,000 tons.

The construction of the craft which used the new waterways is a neglected subject. Some of the standard canal books barely mention them, mainly because few illustrations and even fewer written records have been passed down. In particular, the hull shapes of early barges below the waterline can only be guessed at. Builders didn't work from drawings, but usually from half models from which measurements would be taken, much of the work being done by eye with skills handed down for generations.

The early Wey Navigation craft were probably no more than small swimhead Thames barges. How-

ever, a swimhead barge, shaped like a punt with a sharp right angle at the chine (the jointing between the vertical sides and the flat bottom) had a tendency to dig into the shallow sides of narrow artificially made waterways, and possibly damaged clay linings where they existed. Therefore, by the time of the opening of the Basingstoke Canal in 1794, or even perhaps partly because of it, most barges were constructed with a stem and rounded bow, and, with the influence of the Severn, perhaps with a slightly rounded chine like the trows. The round-stemmed bow, already seen in use on some early Thames barges, was universally adopted for all connecting waterways, and as the larger upper-Thames swim-headed craft could not negotiate the new navigations where much of the trade was to be had, they soon vanished from the river.

The Basingstoke Canal locks were built for barges of similar maximum dimensions to the Wey, and the Kennet and Avon and Grand Junction Canal locks followed suit, so there appears to have been some agreement on a reasonably standardized barge size and capacity, that is about 72ft (22.1m) in length, a

65   Runnymede, c. 1880. Horses tow upstream, and a strangely-shaped narrowboat is assisted downstream by a square-rigged sail

beam of 13ft 9in (4.2m), drawing about $3\frac{1}{2}$ft (1.1m), with a maximum of 80 tons. Alternatively, the locks could have been primarily designed with pairs of Midland narrowboats already in mind, and the barges made accordingly.

WATERWAYS JOINING THE TIDEWAY

The industrial revolution brought about the construction of many canals that were vital to the factories and mines of the Midlands. This rich new area of wealth was linked to the Thames by the Oxford Canal, which opened in 1790. Like many others the Oxford was a narrow canal, with locks built for the standard size of Midland narrowboat 72ft (22m) long by 6ft 10in (2m) wide, carrying between 20 and 30 tons. This size had come about because of the need to conserve water on most artificially made canals, and obviously a small lock

66 Sandford Paper Mills, *c.* 1870. A pair of
narrowboats lie beside the 'Kings Arms' after unloading
coal from the Oxford Canal. The craft behind is the
horse ferry boat

uses much less water than a large one.

The canal was of great benefit to Oxfordshire,
bringing reasonably-priced coal and manufactured
goods to small country wharfs and the City of
Oxford itself. The company hoped that a considerable amount of through traffic down the Thames to
London would ensue, but their hopes were soon to
be dashed. In spite of their bitter opposition, in 1793
the Bill was passed for the building of the Grand
Junction Canal, which by 1800 provided a much
more direct route from the Midlands to London via
the Thames at Brentford.

The Grand Junction was built as a barge canal up
to its junction with the Oxford at Braunston, the
locks being 14ft 6in (4.4m) wide by 80ft (24m) long.
The company's intention was to persuade the
Oxford and other connecting Midland companies to
widen their locks, so that there would be a wide
barge route direct from the coalfields to London.

Unfortunately, this sensible idea was never adopted
and narrowboats, travelling in pairs through the
wide locks, reigned supreme on the through route.
Numbers of 'wide boats' were built for the canal,
but they had to share the southern end with various
styles of small Thames barges.

The Grand Junction built wharfs and warehouses
where the canal joined the Thames at Brentford and
also just above Blackfriars Bridge, so that cargoes
could be unloaded almost in the City. Soon, however, the company withdrew from its Blackfriars
commitment and in 1801 completed a branch line
from Bulls' Bridge, Southall, to Paddington, then a
small village on the western outskirts of London.
There they built a large basin with wharfs and
warehouses, in time to exploit the rapid expansion of
the London suburbs.

Narrowboats and barges carried into Paddington
vast quantities of bricks from the extensive brick-
fields opening up around Hayes and Southall, conveniently on the line of the canal. Other freight
included grain, flour and coal. A certain amount of
sea coal was handled at the southern end of the canal,
but this was soon overwhelmed by cheaper coal

coming down from the Midland collieries. By 1810 Paddington was annually receiving well over 100,000 tons of freight, but despatched west and northwards only about half that amount. London had little to return to the countryside except its waste products, coal ashes, refuse and horse manure, and canal boats were used extensively for this lowly but essential purpose.

In 1820 came the opening of the Regents Canal, a wide waterway connected to the Grand Junction near Paddington and looping around the northern outskirts of the City to join the Pool of London at Limehouse Basin. Here, small ships could unload cargoes such as timber and coal direct into canal barges, for distribution around London and further afield via the Grand Junction. In 1830 Sir George Duckett opened the three mile Hertford Union Canal, which connected his important River Lee Navigation to the Regents at Victoria Park, thereby encouraging a steady growth of trade through London, particularly as large hundred-ton barges could be used on these waterways.

From 1840 the Grand Junction had to compete with vigorous railway competition from the north

67 Caversham Iron Bridge, *c.* 1880. A pair of narrowboats made somewhat unstable by high loads of tree trunks. Long towing lines are slung over convenient projections at the bows. Note the massive Thames barge moored astern and Caversham eel bucks upstream of the bridge

and west, although the railways did in fact bring some business on to the canals locally by building docks at St Pancras on the Regents and at Brentford, Hayes and Southall on the Grand Junction.

For some years the Grand Junction had run its own large fleet of narrowboats, having taken over from some of the original independent carriers such as Pickfords, but in 1876 they decided to pull out of the carrying business. This followed the steady decline in revenue from through traffic, and sudden financial difficulties because of large claims for compensation, following the famous Regents Canal explosion – when the gunpowder cargo on one of several barges towed by a steam tug blew up, killing the crew of three and devastating a large area.

However, in spite of such setbacks the canals survived. New independent carrier fleets such as that

68 Early days at Paddington, 1828. Narrowboats going
in all directions at the junction of the Regent's and
Grand Junction Canals. (T. Shepherd)

of Fellows, Morton and Clayton were formed,
bringing greater efficiency, particularly with the
introduction of steam power on to narrowboats.
Trade was also sustained by the rapid expansion of
industrial estates to the west of London. Factories
were built alongside the canal and many new cut-
tings, up to a mile in length, were dug, leading off
the canal to factory docks, so that raw materials
could be unloaded directly into factory premises.

Between 1929 and 1932 the Grand Junction amal-
gamated with the Regents and a number of Midland
waterways to become the Grand Union Canal Company. A programme of modernization was carried
out, including the widening of locks from Braunston
to Birmingham to take pairs of narrowboats; diesel-
engined lead boats towing unpowered 'butty' boats.

In spite of these attempted improvements,
nothing could stop the general decline of the commercial waterways. By the 1970s working narrow-

boats began to follow other relics of the Industrial
Revolution into new museums devoted to the working past. People can now take a nostalgic look back
at life on 'The Cut', but probably very few can
appreciate how hard the life really was.

Lack of space forbids the brief stories of other
smaller waterways joining London River, but something must be told of the history of one of our most
ancient commercial navigations, the River Lee. This
waterway becomes navigable at Hertford, from
where it flows south for 27 miles by towns such as
Ware, Broxbourne and Enfield to join the Thames
either by the tidal Bow Creek, or the man-made
Limehouse Cut.

The Lee, also spelt Lea, was for centuries an
important highway for the carriage of grain and
malt to London, barge traffic being recorded from at
least the fifteenth century. Improvements in the
form of artificial cuts were being made in Tudor
times, including the construction of the earliest
pound lock in the country with two sets of mitre
gates, built at Waltham Abbey in 1571. Like the
upper Thames it was a source of power for numerous mills, and there were many disputes between

69 Tottenham Mills and Lock, 1839. A busy scene on the Lee Navigation. Labourers with wheelbarrows unloading from small horse-drawn barges. (Marshall)

millers and bargemen over the water supply. Matters improved in the mid eighteenth century, with the digging of further cuts and the construction of pound locks. Similar work was done to make the connecting River Stort navigable up to Bishops Stortford, for the area's premier industry of malting. Coal was carried up for the roasting of barley, and the resulting malt taken back down to London.

Apart from general farm and mill products, gunpowder became one of the most important cargoes carried on the lower part of the Lee. For many years, particularly in time of war, it was taken in special government barges from the long-established explosives factory at Waltham Abbey, down on to the Thames to the Royal Arsenal at Woolwich.

The Lee barges followed a similar pattern of development as those on the Wey, many being horse-drawn up until recent times. The last horse was retired in 1962. But the Lee was a bigger and more open navigation and, as a large number of craft also used the tideway, they were built and rigged as small 'stumpy' spritsail barges. Typical of these was *The Lady of the Lea*; built at Rotherhithe in 1931 for the War Department, with dimensions of 72ft (22m) by 13ft (4m). In recent years she has been rescued from oblivion, loving restored, and is sailing again; the last wooden Thames spritsail barge ever built.

8 *Slow change on the Thames*

THE 1804 BYELAWS

Throughout the centuries pleasure traffic has received short shrift from the professional boatmen. An increase in the number of people using the river for recreational purposes is indicated in the Commissioners' byelaws of 1804. There were complaints by 'Gentlemen and others navigating on the river for pleasure, or otherwise', that they had suffered obstructions, threats and nuisances from bargemasters, costbearers and crews, who could now be fined £10 for any such offence. The byelaw books also included the following regulations for barges.

All barges to be registered with the 'Register of the barges', Zachary Allnutt, at Henley.
Barges to draw a maximum 3ft 10in [1.17m] and have at least 2ft [60cm] of clearboard [freeboard?].
Downward barges were to have preference at locks.
Sails had to be taken down before entering locks.
When a barge was stopped between towpath and navigation channel the mast must be taken down.
That every person towing barges and boats for hire, shall take such barges, boats or vessels in tow, and tow them clear up to the next stage, or place where horses are kept, in course or order, in which they shall come and arrive and shall not give undue preference, or priority to any one barge. Only two flashes per week were allowed below Reading and only when necessary:
The first from Sonning at 12 noon on Wednesday, reaching Boulters at 1 a.m. on Sunday.
The second from Sonning at 3 p.m. on Saturday, reaching Boulters at 4 a.m. on Sunday. Sluices were to be drawn when the water level was at the flash mark or 'at best' near the times laid down. All flood gates and sluices at the locks and mills were to be left open for three hours when the water had dropped to low water mark, and then shut in to bring the water back to 'head'.[1]

INCREASING TRADE

The first half of the nineteenth century saw the peak of barge traffic on English rivers and canals. Soon the livelihoods of many water folk would be swept away before the onslaught of the Railway Age. Had the canals been twice as wide, and the locking system more efficient, perhaps the commercial use of waterways would still be almost as important as on the continent. But it was not to be, and navigations such as the Thames have since lost much of their dignity because of it.

At the beginning of the century the amount of essential goods carried on the Thames's network to and from the swarming Metropolis and southern England averaged 85,000 tons per year, a figure which must have grown as more trade was generated by the new waterways. Total annual cargoes included between 2000 and 3000 cheeses from one upper Thames wharf alone (Buscot), and 20,000 sacks of flour from Reading. From here, a single barge might carry 1200 quarters of malt or other goods to the value of £2000. Hay, wool and cereals, beech in timber and plank, billet wood used as fuel by the London bakers and hoops and brooms from the hazel copses of the Kennet, kept the country wharfs busy with the downward trade. To the valley came roadstone for the new turnpike roads and pottery and hardware from the Midlands down the narrow Oxford Canal, which also brought thousands of tons of coal from the Staffordshire collieries. More coal came from Shropshire and Wales via the Thames and Severn. Canal coal was prevented by statute from going below Reading, because its price competed too well with sea coal from Newcastle

70   Sonning, *c.* 1880. Many barges carried small spritsails at this time. They were not as efficient as the earlier tall square-rigged sails, but were much easier to handle

brought via London docks. Coal could still only be afforded by the more affluent members of English society. The poor still used turf, furze and brushwood for fuel. With the advent of gas lighting, yet further amounts of coal were required for gasworks in riverside towns. Other upward freight included ashes and rags, for manure. The paper mills also needed vast quantities of rags as raw material. Perishable articles were not often carried because of the fear of delays, although they were now infrequent. However, the flash system still had to be used twice a week during drought conditions, even at the new pound locks. By 1809 there were 26 new locks on the river, their dimensions being 110ft (33.5m) × 14ft (4.25m) from Oxford up to Lechlade, and from Oxford down to Windsor 120ft (36.5m) × 18ft (5.5m).

MAVOR'S GENERAL VIEW
The *General View of the Agriculture of Berkshire* by William Mavor, shows that as early as 1809 canal craft may have influenced the design of Thames barges. Swimheaded bows were disappearing and rounded bows were common. It also gives other

information on the crews and their working of a barge.

The construction of barges is almost universally the same, being flat-bottomed, with a rounded head; and as this form is as nearly capable of making speedy way through the water as any other, and as it does not prevent the barge being shoved sideways off the shoals, an inconvenience attending vessels whose heads are differently constructed, it does not appear that any improvement . . . can be made in the shape of the largest barges. [Although the smaller ones might be improved.] It is obvious however that vessels of this description do not easily obey the helm, and therefore the steersman is assisted by bargemen, who, with large ashen poles, from 14 to 19ft in length, with incredible dexterity, keep the barge in the proper navigation channel. The occupation of a bargeman requiring not only strength and activity, but considerable experience and local knowledge, is very lucrative. The number of persons requisite to work the largest barges, is six men and one boy. One of the men, who has the care of the vessel, and who defrays the tonnage, etc., is called cost-bearer, or captain. With the stream downward, these barges require only one horse, with which they travel after the rate of three or three and a half miles in the hour; but against the stream in the upward passage, from 8 to 14 are necessary, according to circumstances.

The Thames Commissioners were entitled to charge four pence per ton toll at their pound locks but the canal companies had persuaded them to reduce to three pence to encourage business. Total tolls at the pound locks for the round trip to Lechlade and back came to 3s 3½d per ton, to which

was added 1s 9d per ton toll at the 32 flash locks still privately owned. Lock-keepers collected the tolls on the upward passage according to the registered tonnage. Half the toll was refunded if the barge returned empty, and a quarter if it was half full. So the barge master or cost-bearer might have to find over £17 for tolls alone on the round trip, as well as the possible two weeks' wage bill for a crew of up to seven. Haulage fees for men or horses had to be paid, and maybe a towpath toll would be demanded by the riparian owners. The cost of haulage of a 128 ton barge upstream could vary from 13 shillings per mile for 14 horses on the swift flowing tideway, to 3s 6d per mile on the Kennet. Sometimes the haulage cost could be negligible, for we must not forget that most vessels were equipped with a sail which was used whenever possible, particularly downstream with the prevailing westerly winds.

The usual time taken from Lechlade downstream to London was five days, from Oxford three-and-a-half, from Reading two and and from Maidenhead one-and-aquarter. Thirty-five miles was a good day's, and sometimes night's, run. This is not a bad figure when one considers that the modern Thames

71 Goring Lock, *c.* 1900. First built in 1787, it was replaced in 1921. The West Country barge is heavily laden with timber, plus the wheels for conveying it on land. Note the set-poles over the bow and the short towing mast. Pity the poor horse which has to haul this load!

powered cruiser takes nine to ten hours for the same mileage, including locking time. The upstream journey took longer, 25 miles on a good day, depending on conditions. Lechlade was usually reached in eight days. The cost of carriage was now £2 per ton for the upward passage and £1 10s down, about $2\frac{1}{2}$ pence per ton/mile. The cost of heavy goods by land was over four times as much, and even on the improving turnpike roads was 1 shilling per ton/mile and could rise to as much as 2s 6d for valuable and perishable goods.

Between 1810 and 1815 there were proposals for canals from the Kennet to Maidenhead and thence to Cowley on the Grand Junction Canal, which had opened in 1805. At long last the City of London was stirred into constructing pound locks to improve the lower river. Six were built on the present sites from

STAINES.—PENTON HOOK LOCK

72 Penton Hook, *c.* 1890. A typical turf-sided lock, first built in 1815, with stout posts to stop barges overriding the lock sides in high water

Teddington to Penton Hook. Bell Weir and Old Windsor came a few years later. By this time many of the up-river timber locks had been rebuilt or patched up on many occasions, owing to the perishable materials used and damage by barges and floods. Gradually they were being replaced by more permanent structures. In 1825 Marlow received a new lock of Headington stone on the present site (to be rebuilt in 1927) and in 1829 a new cut and 'Ray Mill Pound' (only later to be called Boulters) was built at Maidenhead (rebuilt in 1912). The following year Cookham lock and cut were opened at last, by-passing the notorious Hedsor Bend.

CHANGING BARGES

The Act of 1828, relating to the laws and constitution of watermen and lightermen of the tidal river, defined western barges as all flat-bottomed boats and barges navigated from Kingston, or any place beyond, which were allowed to navigate down as far as London Bridge. All vessels used for the carrying of passengers or merchandise had to have the name of the owner, place of abode and the name of the craft painted on the stern in white capital letters and figures, 'the figures not to be less than six inches long, and broad in proportion, and the letters not less than four inches long and broad in proportion.'

By the mid-nineteenth century barge design was continuing to change; 'V' or shallow 'U' vertical transoms replacing the ancient undercut budgett sterns on all barges except tideway lighters and small work punts on the upper river. For centuries barges had been built at small yards in many Thames-side towns and villages, but with the advent of the new style of nineteenth-century barge the builders of the Reading area and the Kennet seem to have been particularly successful. Launchings included a

73 Kingston, *c.* 1870. The ancient royal town was a focus for trade between London and Surrey. A lovely photograph of early 'Stumpy' spritsail barges including an antiquated swimhead. Most tideway barges were soon to carry topsails, a mizzen, and have wheel steering

number of small Thames and Medway spritsail barges, and even trows for the Severn. On the Kennet and Avon Canal at Honey Street near Devizes the firm of Robbins, Lane and Pinniger, founded in 1811, not only built canal barges and small trows but also square-rigged Avon stone barges after the pattern of Thames barges.[2] They also built for the Wey and Basingstoke Canal where until recently it is said some were known as 'Kennet' barges.

Although the basic shape and length to beam ratio may have been similar, craft varied widely in style and details, depending on the waterway and the work to be done. Spritsail barges on coastal work naturally had to be more strongly built than non-

tidal barges and were mainly decked, while the latter had mainly open holds and were decked only at bow and stern. On waterways where low bridges were encountered, cabins were built under the flush decks. The old Western barge collapsible hooped awning or tilt for crew accommodation appears to have gone out with the budgett stern in about 1850. Some of the Tombleson Thames views of 1834 show barges with stern cabins of a similar style to narrow-boats, but of course much more spacious. Similar cabins are seen on craft on the River Avon in illustrations of the Great Western Railway at Bath in 1847 by J. C. Bourne, and therefore we may be looking at what were known as 'Kennet' barges. The style lasted into the twentieth century, and can be seen in paintings by Hazlehurst in Walter Jerrold's *The Silvery Thames* (1906). Of course, on those craft used for short-haul work and the many later towed by tugs, cabins were not often fitted out, but the space under the aft decking could be used if necessary, even on iron barges.

Sails to augment towing were still used on most Thames barges, and sometimes narrowboats, until the end of the nineteenth century. The old square-rigged sail which had predominated had gone by about 1850, having gradually been replaced by small sprit-sails, which appear to have been in use on the non-tidal river from about 1790. Therefore barrel windlasses on the fo'c'sle were still standard equipment for raising and lowering the mast. This was set in a tabernacle, which for square rig had been built on to the floor only slightly forward of centre, but with a spritsail was further towards the bow. Simple sailing beams may also have been used as mast supports.

THE RAILWAY AGE

Despite opposition from many quarters, including the Thames Commissioners and the City of London, Brunel's Great Western Railway Bill was passed in 1834. The line was opened to Maidenhead in June 1838, and two years later reached Reading. The rivers and canals were used extensively to transport

74 Harts flash lock and 'The Anchor' Inn, Eaton Hastings, c. 1865. A sunken barge and luxuriant reed beds illustrate the pre Thames Conservancy dereliction of the upper river. Apart from a small income from lock and inn keeping the proprietor would probably support his family with fishing nets, traps and shot-gun

materials and machinery for the building and running of the G.W.R. In 1837 the first two steam locomotives, *Premier* and *Vulcan*, were sent by sea from Liverpool to London and from thence by barge to West Drayton on the Grand Junction Canal. An elm tree, handily situated at the wharf, was used to support the tackle for lifting the engines from the barge. The famous *North Star* locomotive also came by sea to London docks, but for some unknown reason was sent up the Thames in January 1838, by barge, to Brunel's newly-built Maidenhead railway bridge, there to be put on the western end of the line which then terminated at Taplow. Some writers state that *North Star* stayed on the barge until

75   St John's Lock, Lechlade, 1866. Recently restored by the Thames Conservancy. Previously the river had poured through large holes in the dilapidated gates

May, possibly through a shortage of rails for the line. However, the diary of Daniel Gooch, Brunel's superintendent of the works, tells of no delay, but gives an account of an incident which nearly deprived England of a genius who was yet to create so many marvels.

. . . as I was engaged elsewhere Mr Brunel went to see her unloaded from the barge and very nearly lost his life. There was a heavy chain used as a back guy for the shear legs, and a rope for the opposite one carried across the river. By some mistake this rope was let go and the weight of the chain brought the legs over with a crash, killing one man and just missed crushing Mr Brunel. But for the loss of a man's life I rather rejoiced, after the scolding I had had for doing the work at Drayton without him, that this accident should happen under his supervision, but of course said nothing. . . .[3]

About this time there was a fierce, but shortlived struggle for survival by many of the haulage firms dependent on horses. Not only did stage coach proprietors urge their teams and drivers to make faster and faster journeys, but on rivers and canals in many parts of the country, light 'flyboats' carrying seven to 14 tons, surged on non-stop day and night services with goods and passengers. Three firms ran boats from London as far as Gloucester using double crews and relays of horses, but even these valiant efforts were exhausted by 1840. Despite the railways, however, the increasing population led to ever-increasing transportation of raw materials and manufactured goods, resulting in continuing work for Thames barges, especially in those areas unaffected by the iron roads. Well into the second half of the nineteenth century the river might still carry between one and two hundred barges a week. Many of these would be narrowboats, but a good percentage were the gracefully rounded successors to the swimhead Western barges. Up to the turn of the century and even later; 'Great barges with gaudily

painted sterns were trailed against the stream by slow horses' on the through trade in Oxford, as well as supplying the local needs of farmers, millers and the rest of the riverside population.

Throughout the nineteenth and well into the twentieth century the canal network to the north of the Thames was vital to the rapidly growing industrial areas of the North and Midlands. Apart from the new railways the main trading link with London and its docks was the Grand Junction Canal, which ever since its opening in 1805 had effectively short-circuited much of the traffic from the Oxford Canal. Even so there continued to be a steady flow of narrow boats from the Oxford Canal on to the Thames. Horse-drawn 'worsers', lead boat and butty strapped side by side, sometimes with small square sails set, came silently down from their secret world of narrow waterways, the children wide-eyed at the stately Thames-side mansions and the glittering panorama of London River.

THE THAMES CONSERVANCY

The Act of 1857 gave the first Thames Conservancy body control of the lower river from Staines to the estuary. For a while the old Thames Commissioners still held control of the upper river, until in 1866 a new Act passed the running of the whole river from

76 A Thames Conservancy steam shoal dredger, Twickenham, 1883. An early example of a large number of dredgers which over the years have waged a continuous fight to maintain a navigable depth throughout the length of the river

Cricklade to the sea into the hands of a new, augmented Conservancy. The old Commissioners were said to 'inconveniently numerous' and ill constituted, locks and weirs were in a very bad and dangerous condition, and as tolls were greatly diminished there was insufficient income for repairs. Many workmen had to be laid off and officers worked at reduced salaries, but even so £88,000 was owed. In 1867 Thames Conservancy receipts from lock tolls totalled £2550 from barge traffic and £1020 from pleasure craft.

Any maintenance work the hard-up Thames Commissioners may have done was between Oxford and London, where there was still considerable traffic. The river above Oxford was entirely neglected. Many books and guides of the period, produced for the explosion of interest in Thames pleasure boating, ended their descriptions at Oxford. For most boaters the upper river, with its dilapidated locks, strange little flash locks, fish traps, shoals and water plants from bank to bank – and strange inhabitants – was a place to avoid. Photographs of the stripling Thames round about 1865 graphically show how far back to nature it had gone.

The river soon had a new lease of life when the Conservators of the River Thames took over the whole river in 1866. Within a very few years locks had been rebuilt, some old flash locks removed, and a continuous programme of shoal dredging implemented which lasts until this day.

In 1869 the new Thames Conservancy superintendent for the upper navigation wrote to the Board on the subject of barges driven by steam engines. He stated that two 60 ton craft had recently started operating and now Mr Burmeston of Henley oil-cake mills had added one of 30 tons, plus another of 70 tons. Simmonds, the Reading brewers, had offered to buy one recently built at Blakes Island. Others interested in the new form of propulsion were William Deacon and Co., the wealthy Cook-

ham bankers, brewers and maltsters, who were about to order three to run between Cookham and London.[4]

Despite the advent of the new 'Puffing Billies' the next 20 years show a steady decline of commercial traffic tolls down to £1174 in 1887, but pleasure tolls were steadily rising, in the same year reaching £3805. This may show an increase in the total receipts, but hardly covered the cost of maintaining the river. The new Conservators of the River Thames were given powers to eliminate many of the ancient practices which for so long had interfered with the proper control of the navigation. The Act at last abolished the rights of millers to draw off water, relieved flash lock owners from the obligation to maintain their weirs and abolished the last of the absurd flash lock tolls. Other Acts followed, such as that of 1879, which allowed the Thames Conservancy to charge for water abstraction. The next administrative change came in 1908 when the Port of London Authority took over control of the river below Teddington. In 1974 there was yet another change when, after over a hundred years of river care, the Thames Conservancy became a division of the new Thames Water Authority.

77 Driving piles at Teddington Lock, 1903. A 'T.C.' gang with a pile frame barge completing mooring facilities at the new 650ft (198m) barge lock, built to accommodate a tug towing six barges

78　Teddington, 1903. A wreck raising barge breaks up
the old river wall above the new lock. To the left is the
earlier lock and the almost unique 6ft wide (1.8m) skiff
lock. The first lock was built in 1811 and remained the
lowest on the river until Richmond half tide lock of
1894

79　Harsh conditions, 1929. A tug tows a 'T.C.' gang
to work past Godstow Weir above Oxford. Most lock
and weir stations on the upper river had no road access
until recent times. (*Oxford Journal Illustrated*)

80   The River Inspection, 26 May 1927. Conservancy patrol launches surge up through an immaculate Eynsham flash lock. Work began on the construction of a pound lock in November that year, part of major improvements to the upper river, which came too late for commercial traffic

9 Modern times

KENNET AND AVON DECLINE

The first canal to suffer from the greater carrying capacity and economy of the Great Western Railway was inevitably the Kennet and Avon. The railway reached Newbury in 1847 and only five years later the canal was in a bad state of repair and the company was forced to sell out to the railway. Thereafter the traffic continued to decline, the railway company only doing vital repairs and allowing traffic when it suited them. In 1860 the once thriving Newbury wharf handled less than 7000 tons; in the first decades of the twentieth century the figure had fallen to 3000, about one pair of narrowboats per week.[1]

The principal Newbury carriers at this time were the Ferris family, working with narrowboats and a large wide boat, *Defiance*, built in 1904 by Edward Morgan at Uxbridge on the Grand Junction Canal. She was recorded at Bradford-on-Avon weigh dock as being barrel-sided with crosswise bottom planks and dimensions of 75ft 6in (23m) × 13ft 7in (4.1m), loading 63 tons. Also at Newbury, Dolton had a wide boat *Betty*, built at Uxbridge in 1907, a foot shorter than *Defiance* and with a beam of only 11ft 9½in (3.6m). Up to and during World War II, Chivers had the Wey-type barge *Marjorie*, and narrowboats carrying Simonds beer and Huntley and Palmer biscuits to the docks. After being used for maintenance by Newbury Council, *Marjorie* eventually sank in a basin and was buried when it was filled in.[2]

Meanwhile, towards the western end of the canal, few barge operators found it worthwhile carrying on and through-traffic practically ceased. One exception was the firm of Robbins, Lane and Pin-niger, timber merchants and barge-builders of Honey Street, seven miles east of Devizes, who until 1933 continued to operated a pair of narrow or 'fly' boats, and their 60 ton barge *Unity*, which carried general goods, fertilizers and imported timber between Bristol Docks and Honey Street, and occasionally eastwards to Newbury. *Unity* was built by Robbins in 1896, with dimensions of 67ft (20.6m) by 13ft 6in (4.1m). She appears to have been built on very similar lines to the Wey barges, although the 'D' of the transom stern was much flatter. Two and sometimes three horses were needed for towing when laden.

The story of the 1950 closure of the Kennet Navigation by the Inland Waterways Executive while there was a boat rally at Newbury is well known. The closure seriously affected recently established Newbury narrowboat operators John Gould (who had a contract to carry turf down the Thames to Hampton parish wharf for the Harrison Chaplin nurseries) and John Knill, carrying salt from Cerebos Ltd at Northwich, Cheshire, via the Oxford Canal and Thames to Newbury Laundry. Knill managed to fulfil his contract by unloading later cargoes of salt at Reading and sending them by road transport. He also completed John Gould's turf contract down the Thames, returning to Northwich via Brentford and the Grand Union Canal, picking up any cargoes he could find on the way.

The Kennet and Avon Canal Trust which originated at this time is still making efforts to open up this beautiful waterway, which saw hardly any powered craft. The abundant wild life, which has been unmolested for half a century, before long will be driven out by the thundering diesel engines and

The Canal. Newbury.
No 5132

81 Newbury, *c.* 1920. The sinking wide boat is *Defiance*, which became a permanent feature until broken up in 1980. Behind is Wey barge *Marjorie*, plus an unknown wide boat with fore-cabin

pollution of modern pleasure craft.

THAMES AND SEVERN DECLINE

The Thames and Severn Canal had always suffered from serious leakage of water through the porous limestone of the Cotswolds, and in the latter part of the nineteenth century diminishing traffic returns because of railway competition left no money for expensive repairs. A canal which had seen nearly 2000 barges pass in a year, by the 1880s saw but a few.

A book of west-bound toll tickets dating from December 1882 to December 1883 issued at Lechlade wharf, now in the Gloucester Record Office, gives the names of passing barges, together with owners, steerers and customers, the merchandise carried, and its destination. The cargoes mainly comprised wheat, oats and barley, some certainly from local farms, destined for Chalford, Stroud and Gloucester. Timber was also delivered to Stroud Valley firms. The struggling Thames and Severn Canal Company

was still the biggest barge owner with *Victory*, *Edith*, *Hugh Percy*, *Excelsior*, *Hope* and *Victoria*, altogether making 23 trips in three years. James Smart of Chalford completed a few trips with *Beatrice*, *Kate* and *Floorey*. Solo trips were made by a few other firms and W. Smith's *Trial* did four. The Canal Company was almost matched with 21 cargoes by Lechlade's Matthew Hicks in his narrowboat *Good Intent*.

However, the canal continued to die, and by 1893 James Smart of Chalford was receiving letters from Mr Tovey, a Lechlade seedsman, as follows:

I have had an invoice of the 50 quarters of Barley bought at Sharpness ex. *The Austria* so presumably the vessel is now in port. Be sure and take it in during the long days.

A month later he wrote:

Please let me know when I shall receive the 50 quarters of Barley put in your boat some weeks ago and oblige.

Stronger words came from flour Mill owners Kemble and Dash of Stroud:

We shall be glad to know what you propose to allow us on the 200 sacks of wheat just delivered up from Lechlade. Eight weeks in transit is not to be endured, and as this is

not by any means the first time we have had to complain of delay, we must insist now on your calling and making some arrangement with us. We cannot think of ordering any more grain by water from the district above us on the canal. Yours Truly.[3]

Household states that some repairs were carried out and the canal re-opened in 1899. The narrowboat *The Trial* was chartered from James Smart and eventually brought a cargo of wood from London. But soon major leaks again forced the closure of the summit level and, although in later years repairs allowed a trickle of craft through, the major restoration schemes came to nothing and the canal was abandoned in 1927. The old locks lie as quietly crumbling monuments to a golden canal age in the Golden Valley.

THE WEY AND BASKINGSTOKE BARGES

The River Wey, one of the earliest navigations in England to be improved with pound locks, outlasted in commercial terms many of its counterparts. This was because of its close proximity to London as a wide, easily maintained navigation, with a plentiful

82 Lechlade, 1882. The Thames and Severn Canal Company wharf at almost the highest navigable point on the river for large craft. Matthew Hicks's narrowboat *Good Intent* waits for a cargo for the canal

and inexpensive water supply. From 1794 it connected with the Basingstoke wide canal, which encouraged trade and brought extra tolls. It was also the highway for the successful trading firm of William Stevens and Sons, who built their first barge at Guildford in 1840.

From at least 1830 considerable amounts of gunpowder were carried down the Wey and Thames from the Chilworth factory just south of Guildford, to government arsenals such as at Barking in Essex. The factory owner, Samuel Sharpe, for a long time had his own barges, but from the 1880s until 1916 William Stevens took over the barging side of the business.[4]

The Wey barges, capable of carrying over 80 tons, although towed by tugs in their final days, were the ultimate development of centuries of wooden barges on the Thames and its connecting waterways; the last barges trading 'West Country'. Some, such as the Robbins-built *Perseverance*, carried in the 1880s small sprit-sails, but often horses had to be hired for towage to Teddington, and tugs used on the tideway.

Although building many of their own, from at least the 1880s Stevens were ordering barges from Robbins, Lane and Pinniger on the Kennet and Avon Canal. In 1891 they quoted £315 for a barge with elm bottom, oak sides and pitch-pine keelson. In this instance iron knees were fitted. The price included delivery to Reading. An undated notebook found at Guildford includes a sketch and measurements, possibly by Mr Stevens, for the barge *Industry*. It gives a beam of 13ft 8in (4.15m) and an overall length of 73ft 3in (22.35m), made up of a foredeck measuring 11ft 8in (3.56m), 50ft (15.25m) of stowage under hatches, a 3ft 11in (1.20m) companionway between bulkheads, and 7ft 8in (2.34m) for the after cabin.[5]

83 Wey barge *Speedwell* at Ellesmere Port Museum, 1985. Stern view with rudder un-pinned and folded back

All inland craft were subject to the Canal Boats Act of 1877, which laid down the minimum amount of 'free air space' for each person in the cabin. Wey barges such as *Speedwell* (now at the Boat Museum, Ellesmere Port), registered with the Port of London Authority in 1925, were allowed to have only two persons sleeping in the cabin. Access to the cabin was via a sliding hatch on the afterdeck. Inside, there were bunks, built-in cupboards and an iron stove. The sides of the barge were held rigid by tension chains and cross-beams, which also provided support for the waterproof hatches covering the hold — essential when grain was being transported. A barrel windlass was set low between bitts on the foredeck. It was used for the anchor when this was needed on the tideway, and sometimes for warping alongside ships in the docks. The rudder was hinged and held by a pin, and therefore could be swung back flush with the stern to clear lock gates and cills. The tiller, like the windlass, was almost flush with the deck to clear low bridges, and there was a lower section of decking above the companionway on which the steersman stood. The sides of the barge were painted

black, but Stevens outlined the coaming sides in green and the white transom was edged with red.

In the 1920s Stevens's *Speedwell* and her sister-barges were carrying up cargoes such as maize from Canadian ships in the Surrey Commercial Docks, and taking away flour from Coxes Mill above Weybridge. At this time Whittet and Company had their own barge, *Scot*, carrying away drums of linseed oil from the Ham Oil Mills, just above Thames Lock. The 1935 barge book from Thames Lock, where the canal joins the river, shows that Stevens's barges were carrying over 80 tons of wheat each from London to Coxes Mill, and C. W. Beckett's barges were taking battens and boards on to the Basingstoke Canal. A. J. Harmsworth was carrying linseed grains to Ham Mills and up to 90 ton loads of coal on to the Basingstoke, much of it probably to Woking gas works. With this tonnage the canal could cope with a substantial barge draught of 4ft 6½in (1.40m).

In the twentieth century the firm of A. J. Harmsworth was the main carrier on the Basingstoke Canal. Some of their early barges came from Costains on the Grand Junction Canal and Robbins on the Kennet and Avon. It is said that 'they took the lines off' Robbins's barge *Glendower* when they started building their own craft at Ash Vale in 1918. Alec Harmsworth also built the steam-tug *Shamrock* for towing on the river, but on the canal two horses were most often used. Harmsworths continued building barges similar to the Wey craft until 1935, one of the last being *Aldershot*, finally demolished at West Byfleet in 1984. Only wooden barges were made, with flat bottoms of 2½in (6cm) pine. Frames, vertical sides and slightly rounded chines were made of oak. The stern was the familiar 'D' shape and the stem vertical on the bluff bows, rounding under the waterline to join the flat bottom. Inside the stowage area all barges were sheathed with deal on bottom and sides. The repair business at Ash Vale ceased in 1947 after the closure of the canal.[6]

The carriage of linseed to Ham Mills ceased in 1963 when the mills burnt down. Thereafter, practically the only trade was to Coxes Mill with grain

84 The hold of *Speedwell* with cross beams and tension chains

from the docks. Harmworths, with *Fleet*, were still on this trade with eight of Stevens's barges, *Diligent, Kate, Victory, Renown, Reliance, Hope, Perseverance IV* and *Speedwell*. In 1969, when the grain terminal was moved down to Tilbury, Mr Stevens retired, and the five remaining craft were sold as house and maintenance boats. The Wey Navigation was taken into the care of the National Trust. There is a very active Basingstoke Canal Society working enthusiastically to re-open that very useful waterway.

Two Wey barges, *Speedwell*, registered in 1925, and *Perseverance IV*, 1937, were rescued by far-sighted members of the Society for Spritsail Barge Research. *Speedwell* was taken into the care of the Boat Museum, Ellesmere Port, and *Perseverance IV* sent to the new Docklands Musuem.

It may have been a Wey or Basingstoke barge, renamed *Firebrand*, that on 10 June 1960 hit the headlines of the *Wiltshire and Gloucester Standard*, by being the first horse-drawn craft to reach Lechlade for 40 years. *Firebrand* had been converted into a

kind of hotel-cum-camping boat and worked for two seasons with fortnightly trips between Abingdon and Lechlade. Lyn David, the lock-keeper at St John's, knew well beforehand when it was coming up the river, when irate farmers telephoned to complain that their (illegal) barbed wire fences across the towpath had been cut to let the horse through. The horse didn't particularly care for the job and sometimes wandered off in the night and the holiday party would spend a happy morning trying to catch it. One day it went on strike, right in the middle of the boardwalk across Rushey Weir. After several hours of pushing and pulling, the Fire Brigade and an R.S.P.C.A. vet were called. After the horse was safely moved to firm ground the vet gave it two weeks' sick leave.

In the early 1980s T. and D. Murrell made a last bid (for the present) to keep wide barge commerce alive on the freshwater Thames; once again exercising the east- and west-about concession, carrying grain from Tilbury Grain Terminal to Coxes Mill with motorized barges *Clinton* and *Annie*, the latter skippered by Keith Tagg, from a very well known Thames family. After delivering her final 70 tons

85   Bow of *Speedwell* with low barrel windlass and bitts

Annie left the Wey on 20 May, 1983.

THAMES TRADE CONTINUES

In 1905 the river above Staines carried over 70,000 tons, much of it going to and from the associated waterways such as the Wey and Oxford Canal, but a considerable amount was made up of fairly localized horse-drawn barge traffic on the higher reaches, such as the carriage of corn out of the Vale of the White Horse to Reading from wharfs at Sutton Courtenay and elsewhere. But already the mechanical age had disturbed the placid reaches of the upper river. There were screw-driven steam barges and also steam tugs which were regularly used to tow dumb barges up as far as Oxford. Steam-barges in service in the 1920s included *London Stone*, *Divers Companion* and *Ambition*. The latter regularly carried about 50 tons of imported grain from London to various mills, sometimes returning with beer from Simmonds Brewery at Reading. Emmanuel Smith's barges, *Swan*, *Chinaman*, *Laford* and *Boldsford*, transported timber, coal and other merchandise, towing six barges below Teddington, four to Molesey, and three to Bray: a maximum of two was allowed above Bray. Many planks 'fell' overboard, giving rise to a rash of new riverside sheds and apparently even bungalows! In 1926 the Thames Conservancy Secretary had to issue the following instruction to lockstaff:

Complaints have been received from firms trading upon the river that a serious leakage occurs during transit between the point of loading and the point of discharge of commodities such as coal, timber, etc., and all lock-keepers are directed to assist, as far as they are able, to detect any interference with cargoes while vessels are in the vicinity of their locks, and to report any cases of pilfering or unauthorized removal of any goods from barges. Lock-keepers, weir-keepers and ferrymen are particularly warned against receiving or purchasing from persons in charge of craft, any merchandise whatsoever, and any case of a Conservator's employee so doing, will be severely dealt with.[7]

Midland narrow boats from the Oxford Canal continued to supply coal to riverside wharfs at Benson and elsewhere, to mills such as Wolvercote and Sandford, and also brought down mass-produced pottery from Staffordshire and others goods from the Midlands. In the 1920s the Thames Conservancy average annual merchandise figures for traffic above Teddington amounted to about 350,000 tons. There

was a continuous programme of navigation improvements throughout the river, including in 1928 the rebuilding of Godstow lock, the removal of Medley flash lock, and the replacing of Kings and Eynsham flash locks with new pound locks. This reopened the river above Oxford, which had become so awkward that the few canal boats which used the upper Thames had always bypassed Godstow reach via the canal and Dukes Cut. Kings weir had been particularly difficult, being probably unique in having as a passage-way a single pair of mitre gates similar to pound lock gates, instead of paddle and rymer tackle.

THE KINGSTON DISASTER

The Thames Valley in the late 1920s suffered from exceptionally severe frosts and floods. In previous decades the popularity of pleasure boating and increasing affluence had induced speculators to build acres of riverside bungalows and other desirable residences on the flood plain, and the newspapers were full of descriptions of hardship and complaints about flooding. The illustrious and much respected Lord Desborough, Chairman of the Conservancy for 32 years, replied to the effect that if people built on the flood-plain they should expect to get flooded out. The Conservancy was not responsible for flood prevention and when there was exceptional rainfall a channel twice the size of the present one would be needed to prevent it.

The floods in January 1928 brought probably the greatest catastrophe to commercial traffic, apart from the World War II blitz, ever experienced on the Thames. The *Daily Chronicle*'s story on January 3rd is worth quoting:

TEDDINGTON, Tuesday night.
A fantastic armada of about 20 fully-laden barges careering down the Thames between Kingston and Teddington this afternoon threatened the town of Richmond with flooding that might well have been catastrophic.... Tonight the spectacle at Teddington Lock is a remarkable one. Its still waters are occupied by eight or ten barges laden with great stacks of timber. Across one part of the weir lies an upturned 'monkey boat', or small barge, which has strewn its cargo in all directions. At another part of the weir lie three laden barges, broadside on to the raging waters.

All are obstructions to the discharge of the flood water which hourly increases in pressure. Inside the lock there floats wreckage of all descriptions. In addition to the barges there are two steam launches, which were forced to race when the barges started their mad progress...

For two hours it seemed as though the Thames had gone mad. Barges at the Town End Wharf were the first to break away with the constantly-swelling waters. A hawser snapped like string, and the barges quickly freed themselves from their ropes and charged towards the bridges.

Several of them, owned by the Mayor of Kingston (Mr T. C. Smith) and by Mr C. W. Beckett, cleared the arches of the solid stone bridge, but three or four crashed into the arches, two of which are almost completely blocked. At least two of the barges – one a coal boat carrying 180 tons – went down, or, at least, are just visible as wrecks, with their timber cargoes heaped up against the bridge.

The runaways that swept through the arches gained great momentum and collided with other barges. Whistles, sirens, telephones got to work. Tugs were mobilised with incredible swiftness and chased the barges, each a menace to anything in their path, practically all carrying

100 tons. The railway bridge came in the way, and eight of the barges crashed into it. *Just two minutes later a train passed over this rather fragile-looking bridge at normal speed.*

It was here that the tugs came in. They danced about the runaways and got hawsers aboard and lugged the runaways back to Kingston. But the other truants were still heading for the weir and urgent preparations were made to meet the assault.

By skilful manoeuvring they were kept from crashing with full force into the lock. Fortunately, it was the empty barge that got there first, and, by acting as a buffer, saved the situation. In that last sweep a number of motor launches paid penalty for being in the way, and now lie at the bottom.

Lord Desborough later stated that on that day no fewer than 26 barges broke loose. The first was at Romney, laden with timber, and she got across the weir, but the Conservancy staff, working hard, got her away by 10 o'clock. Then later on, by various mischances which would no doubt be inquired into in the future, there were no fewer than 25 barges loose at Kingston. The Engineer telephoned to him,

86 Kingston Bridge, 3 January 1928. Lighters and barges form a log-jam in the bridge arches

and he gave instructions that no expense was to be spared in trying to secure the barges. They employed all their own tugs and commandeered others, in an exciting chase to capture the barges, but Lord Desborough was sorry to say that three were still sunk near Kingston Bridge. He wished to pay a tribute to the men who, at considerable risk to their lives and at the cost of very hard work, helped to prevent such a catastrophe as would have resulted from the barges going over Teddington Weir. Two of Mr Tough's men rendered invaluable service, and Captain Parr and the tug *Ham* performed prodigies. They were also indebted to the Mayor of Kingston, Mr Beckett, and others for most valuable assistance. Two houseboats he knew were sunk, and one launch went through Teddington weir and had not been seen or heard of since. Another launch sank in Teddington lock cut, but had since been raised.[8]

The reason why so many barges had escaped from Kingston was that the traffic had outstripped the mooring facilities (the maximum number of barges requiring berths between Kingston and Teddington was later given as 86). Timber barges were moored three and four abreast at the wharfs and the cables couldn't take the strain of the floodwaters. Thirty thousand tons of imported timber was said to be handled annually at Kingston wharf, and 10,000 tons at Hampton Wick. It was distributed throughout the valley by smaller barges or lorries.

STEAM AND DIESEL

Other trade at the time included raw materials, such as rags for paper-making which were brought to Taplow, Temple and other paper mills, and imported grain, which went to corn mills such as Marsh and Sonning. Another short-lived attempt by

87 Rescuing sunken barges at Kingston, 3 January 1928. There have been many unsung heroes among the river gangs, who sometimes perform seemingly impossible tasks often in dangerous conditions like these

a miller to use the river commercially was made in 1959 when grain for chicken feed was brought direct from London Docks to Marsh Mills in two days.

From the 1930s Samuel Beckett's tugs, *Vim*, *Pep*, *Pygmy*, *Puffin* and *Bess*, towed special Dutch-built steel barges on regular runs to the great timber yards at Marlow, Reading and Oxford. Not only did some of the tugs have quite comfortable living accommodation for a week away from home, but the long tradition of a semi-nomadic river life was also perpetuated on the great hundred-ton barges where cramped quarters were provided under the stern deck for a couple of bargemen, or sometimes man and wife. The immaculate tugs, towing two smart barges stacked high with imported softwood, must have made a brave show as they swept up the river. Sometimes a tank barge might be dropped off at Maidenhead gasworks wharf on the way up, filled

with gas oil, and picked up a few days later as the tug left Boulters lock on the way back towards London.

Two of the largest steam tugs working on the non-tidal river were *Thames* and *Black Prince*. Both were on Thames Conservancy maintenance work until the late 1930s or early 40s. *Black Prince* was about 70ft (22m) long and could carry about 20 tons forward of the cabin and engine room. The funnel was let down on a counterweight to negotiate the bridges. The Conservancy had other tugs, including *Bourne* and *Cherwell*, and gradually built up a large fleet of wooden and later steel barges, working flats and some narrowboats for lock and weir building and maintenance, and also steam dredgers which gradually replaced hand-dredging equipment. Some tugs later had petro/paraffin engines fitted, but on some steam engines continued to be used until the 1950s, when many tugs were converted to diesel engines or replaced by motor tugs.

During World War II, Simmonds Brewery at Reading made a valuable contribution to the war

88 Kingston Bridge, 3 January 1928. Rescuers relax on the massive battered bows of barge *Connaught*

effort by exporting beer to the troops overseas. A regular barge-load of barrels would leave Reading *en route* for the docks and weave its erratic, aromatic way down-river, miraculously steered by a barge-man nonchalantly leaning on the tiller because he was too drunk to stand up. Lucky was the lock-keeper who had the barge tied to his layby over-night! At least one company exercised the right to 'the east- and west-about concession', whereby West Country boatmen could navigate through the Pool of London without having to be accompanied by a licensed waterman, a concession reputed to have been granted by Charles II because of the bargemen's help to the population of London during the Great Plague. The war effort was also helped by firms such as E. C. Jones, of Brentford, who carried timber up to Reading, with a maximum of 32 barge-loads in 1941.

Throughout World War II Odell's tugs, *Leo*, *Rennie*, *Oxford*, *Oval* and *Odette* were a common sight on the river as far as Oxford; the latter two in

particular did at least 30 trips, towing one or more barges loaded with R.A.F. stores to Abingdon. The trips are recorded in a surviving barge toll book from one of the local locks, dating from 1941 to 1956. Many other military barge trips are noted, but never the contents or tonnage, which was presuma-bly toll-free. Some were steel 76-ton barges from the Grand Union Canal, with no-nonsense names such as *Hayestwig* and *Hayesoak*; others were *Stock*, *Awe*, *Peat*, *Thorn* and *Board*. Some worked through the lock singly and therefore may have been steam or motor barges. Altogether nearly 70 barge loads were delivered to Abingdon between September 1942 and October 1944. In the same period over 20 pairs of named Fellows, Morton and Clayton narrowboats,

89   Thames Conservancy steam tug *Black Prince*, 18 February 1929, with an empty barge on tow, breaking ice in Boulters lock cut

90 Streatley, 1935. In the afternoon sunshine, Thames
Conservancy tug *Cherwell* tows a barge rapidly
upstream towards Goring lock

mainly from the Oxford Canal but a few from
Brentford, delivered mainly similarly unidentified
cargoes to Moulsford and Benson wharfs. No other
commercial cargoes are noted, except in May 1944,
when four pairs of narrowboats carried a total of 165
tons of copper, then a very valuable commodity,
through from Brentford to Oxford. The same
month two pairs carried 80 tons of steel in the other
direction. From 1944 little further commercial traffic
is noted in this area, the main exception being
between September 1949 and June 1951, when John
Knill with narrowboat *Columba*, later augmented
with *Kenelm*, made a few journeys carrying salt to
Newbury and Reading from Cerebos Ltd at Northwich in Cheshire, via the canal system.

The merchandise figures for the river above

Teddington almost doubled during the war, reaching over 600,000 tons in 1944. The average of about
300,000 tons per annum was maintained into the
1950s. In March 1952 Becketts took their last
hundred-ton barge load of grain to Sonning Mill.
Several lock maintenance closures over a period of
three months then closed the river for through
traffic. The mill then had to bring in road transport
which was found to be more economical, and the
lorries stayed. Thereafter there was a very rapid
decline in trade above Teddington and by the early
1970s most commercial traffic had ceased to the
Wey, and even to the great timber wharfs at Hampton Wick and Kingston. Samuel Beckett's had sold
their tugs, some staying on the Thames with Aubrey
Watson's, the dredging contractors. In 1972 the
merchandise figures barely reached 4000 tons.

In the 1980s the surviving carrying trade on the
upper Thames has been the narrowboats of the firm
of Ashby Canal Transport Ltd, followed by the

Metropolitan and Midland Canal Trading Company, bringing coal once or twice a year from the midlands via the Oxford or Grand Union canals to supply lock-keepers and other riverside dwellers who might find it difficult to obtain coal in any other way.

Some of the very specialized ancient skills needed to move large cumbersome barges on the confined waters of the Thames are still passed on, sometimes from father to son, among the dredging contractor gangs, and the maintenance and dredger crews, tugmen and bargemen employed by the Thames Conservancy; now called the Rivers Division of the Thames Water Authority. Even if there is never a return of heavy commercial traffic on the Thames, many maintenance jobs will always have to be done with the help of barges, and the skills to move them, in all river conditions, from drought to flood, will still be needed.

10 The Tidal Thames

ROMAN LONDON

Soon after the successful invasion in AD 43, the Roman army established a supply base at what was to become Londinium, then the probable upper limit of high tides.[1] The rapid subjugation of Southern Britain soon allowed trading links to be established with the British tribes and with the rest of the Roman Empire, and it was found that the site was ideal for a permanent trading settlement. The river provided a sheltered anchorage, with easy access seawards to the continental trade routes and access upstream with river barges to the interior of the island.

In spite of the sacking and burning of the infant city by Boudicca in AD 61, it was soon re-established and continued to grow. Administrators and planners moved in, and stately stone and brick houses and public buildings rose above the ancient landing beaches. Smaller timber houses of artisans and merchants began to spread along the waterfront, and the army engineers were brought in to construct great timber revetments and jetties along the foreshore so that merchants from many lands could moor their ships.

The first Roman London Bridge across the Thames, sited slightly downstream of the modern bridge, had probably been built before AD 100. It is thought that the closely-set wooden piles of this bridge obstructed the passage of the largest sea-going ships, and therefore the main quays for the city developed in the Billingsgate area just below the bridge, a pattern that was followed after the building of the medieval bridge a thousand years later. There would have been many other quays and warehouses spreading along the waterfront for smaller barges from up-river, which were bringing in building materials and farm produce from the Thames Valley.

Several small ships or barges of Roman date have been found in the bed of London River, representing a wide range of craft built for varying purposes. The largest was found in 1910 during the construction of County Hall. From the excavated remnants it was deduced that she was a decked sea-going cargo vessel about 70ft (21m) in length, and probably of Mediterranean origin. In 1958 a fragmented 50ft (15m) craft was found during the construction of a new surgical block of Guys Hospital. As the sides of this craft were only about one metre high it is thought that it was a flat-bottomed river barge, incapable of sailing in rough water. Thirdly, in 1962, a more robust double-ended flat-bottomed barge was discovered two metres below the bed of the river between the Blackfriars bridges, just upstream of the limits of the Roman city. This was a 50ft (15m) decked barge, with a mast step, and could therefore be sailed. She had been carrying a cargo of Kentish ragstone, some of which still lay in the remains of the hold. All these craft were made of oak, the latter two at least probably locally constructed, as Celtic techniques had been used.[2]

In two centuries Londinium grew into the greatest trading and administrative city in Britain. Objects of the Roman period discovered in excavations came from as far away as Greece, Turkey, Syria and North Africa. Defensive walls were not built on the landward side until the early third century, and the river frontage, nearly a mile in length, appears to have been undefended for an even longer period. It was not until about AD 370 that a massive riverside wall was built behind the wharfs and quays, approximately on the line of modern Thames Street. This wall, long suspected by some, but not discovered until 1975, was obviously to protect the city from the Saxon sea-going marauders who were now threatening much of the coast of the soon-to-be abandoned province of Brittania.

SAXON LONDON

The political and economic chaos leading up to the fall of the empire meant that Londinium was to collapse as a port and trading centre, but as in other parts of Britain, a small population of Romano-Britains seemed to have kept some sort of Romanized town life in being into the fifth century. It is thought that London was never entirely abandoned during the Dark Ages, and that in the sixth and seventh centuries the large numbers of Saxon settlers who were moving up the Thames valley found the crumbling ruins of London just as suitable for a port as other sailors had centuries before.

The slow submergence of the land over this long period meant that by now the tidal limits were probably well above London. The early Roman levels were now submerged and even the great riverside defence wall was being undermined by high tides. The Saxons flattened or let fall the ruins of Roman London and began to build their own less sophisticated but more vigorous city on top of the rubble. London once again began to grow as a centre of trade, competing with other ports founded as trading emporia such as Ipswich and Hamwith, near Southampton, and there were once again strong connections with the Rhineland.

The early flat-bottomed clinker-built Saxon ships needed no quays for loading and unloading cargoes but could be run up on to the sloping beaches now overlying the old Roman shore installations. Some of these beaches, reaching as high as the base of the old city wall, may have been artificially constructed flood banks to stem the rising tides. Ships of the Frisians, then the most successful traders of north-west Europe, would have been frequent visitors, one of the most common cargoes being slaves. By the tenth century London was a major centre of international trade.

Even the numerous Viking attacks in the ninth and tenth centuries, when great fleets of longships lay in the Thames estuary, and London itself was sacked and occupied on several occasions, did not stop trade with Europe. Many Scandinavian merchants resided peaceably in the city, and their ships, similar to those depicted on the Bayeux Tapestry, continued to slip across the Channel when it was known that the Viking warships were plundering elsewhere. The steady growth of seaborne trade, particularly to the Baltic region, meant that larger sailing ships were needed, and the Frisians and others slowly developed large flat-bottomed beamy cargo vessels with high sides and square-rigged sails, known generally as cogs.

MEDIEVAL GROWTH

The first wharf property on the London waterfront to be recorded by name was Queenhithe, known from AD 889. This became one of the most important royal properties above the later London Bridge, and was to develop into a large rectangular sheltered inlet on the otherwise largely un-indented frontage. Billingsgate is also known to have been an important wharf from about AD 1000. Its merchandise records from that time cover wood, wool, cloth, pigs, spices and fish. As the medieval city grew, other parts of the waterfront were acquired for the establishment of specialist wharf areas such as the Vintry for the Anglo-Norman wine trade, and the Steelyard, a trading centre of the Cologne merchants from at least AD 1170. Apart from the wharfs with their granaries and warehouses, the waterfront was soon taken up with shops, taverns and various trades and crafts including fishmongers, brewers, dyers, coopers, carpenters and metal workers.[3]

All the time the tide was getting higher, but instead of withdrawing from it, traders started to push out into the river. Along nearly the whole length of the city waterfront individuals started to protect their property from the tides with vertical timber revetments. These were back-filled with spoil to make level working areas which were also suitable for the erection of new buildings nearer the water's edge. We can visualize that as soon as one wharfinger had finished building a new frontage then his neighbour, seeking to grab the passing river traffic from him, would start driving piles further out in the river.

Narrow passageways ran between properties and stairs led on to the foreshore so that people could

91   Tideway scenes in 1802. Above is a cutter-rigged
Kentish hoy laden with ships' stores, and below a
spritsail straw barge and a massively constructed lime
barge being re-pitched. (W. H. Pyne)

reach the river to do their laundry, collect water and
board boats. By the sixteenth century much of the
waterfront had moved southwards into the river by
at least 330ft (100m). In places there are a series of no
fewer than 12 buried medieval timber or stone
revetments marching out into the river. The depth
of accumulated deposits over the ancient Roman
levels today totals about 33ft (10m).

LONDON BRIDGE

London Bridge was soon to be the most prominent
feature of the bustling river scene. The earlier
Roman bridge across to Southwark had almost
certainly disintegrated in the Dark Ages. Several
chroniclers relate that later wooden bridges existed
in the eleventh and twelfth centuries, but these were
apparently not very substantial structures. But in
1176 Peter of Colechurch began the construction of
the famous London Bridge, which took 33 years to

complete and was to last for 600 years.

It had a most unusual appearance from the beginning. There were 19 unequal pointed stone arches
founded on groups of enormous piles driven into the
riverbed. On top of the piles thick planks formed a
platform set in pitch from which the arches sprang.
Over the centuries these wooden piers or 'sterlings'
needed constant repair, with more and more piles
being added, until the sterlings grew to grotesque
proportions with very little room through some
arches for the tide to flow. Some arches at either end
were even stopped up with corn mills and water
wheels for pumping water into the city. The whole
structure acted like a gigantic weir, and towards the
end of its life, with tides now reaching inland higher
than Teddington, there could be a fall of five feet
(1.5m) through the bridge at the ebb of the tide. The
noise of the rushing waters could be heard all over
the city.

Navigation became extremely hazardous. Most
boatmen with any sense only went through at slack
water, and even then there was the chance that at
high tide a barge or ship could get trapped on top of
one of the sterlings which were then covered with

water. Accidents were frequent to small craft, and large ones were not immune from damage. For instance, in 1795 a large West-Indiaman broke free from its moorings and was driven upstream by the tide into the large central arch where all its masts were broken off at deck level, was forced through the arch and continued up the river as far as Somerset House! Three years later a spritsail hay barge drove against the bridge with great velocity, the mast not being lowered in time. It struck the balustrading over the central arch, and some of the stonework which fell killed two of the crew.[4]

From its earliest days the bridge had a large stone chapel placed on the great central pier. To this were soon added other timber-framed buildings, some as much as five storeys high, until the whole structure took on the appearance of a city street. The rear portion of the houses and shops, hanging out over the river, were described as being '... broken by hanging closets and irregularities (which) offer a very disgusting object ... and seem to lean as to fill the beholder with utter amazement and horror.' Another feature of the bridge from an early date was the drawbridge, positioned over the 30ft (9m) wide gap between the thirteenth and fourteenth piers from the north end. At first it was used extensively to allow cargo ships laden with corn and fish to reach the royal wharf at Queenhithe, west of the bridge, but as ships grew too large to get through, then Billingsgate below the bridge became the main entry dock and goods were transferred to carts or lighters to go westwards. By at least the eighteenth century, according to the Strype 1756 edition of Stow's *Survey of London*, the drawbridge had ceased to be used. All small sailing craft using the bridge arches had to have masts set in tabernacles so that they could be dropped easily.

The last houses on old London Bridge were not demolished until 1762, but the bridge itself survived in a cleaned-up but dangerous state until its demolition in 1834, three years after the opening of Rennie's new London Bridge. If it had not been for old London Bridge the whole aspect of the waterfront may have been different, at least until the eighteenth century, with merchantmen and fishing fleets moving up to anchorages on the western side of the city. Instead, the 'Pool' of London, the anchorage below bridges, came into being at an early date, leading to the eventual establishment of Dockland.

THE HIGHWAY OF LONDON

Until the eighteenth century there was no bridge apart from London Bridge crossing the tidal river until one reached Kingston, 20 miles upstream. Therefore passengers and goods travelling between London and Thames-side villages south of the river but away from the bridge were invariably carried by ferry boats. Indeed, the general inconvenience of travelling over very poor roads meant that river transport was preferred to reach places on the north bank also. As the population of London grew throughout the Middle Ages it generated a colossal amount of localized river traffic taking passengers and goods along the river both east and west. Daily cargoes of fish and farm and garden produce were brought to numerous city wharfs, which by the sixteenth century were equipped with cranes. In 1593 John Norden wrote of the inhabitants of Middlesex who lived near the river that '... they live either by the barge, by the wherry or ferry, by the sculler or by fishing, all which live well and plentifully, and decent and honest sort relieve their families.'

Apart from the Western barges moving down to Queenhithe from the upper reaches, little is known about the early river craft which were used for the carrying trade on the tidal Thames. However, some information has been gleaned from fragments of two medieval boats excavated at Blackfriars. Both were of oak clinker construction, one having been carrying a cargo of building stone from Maidstone, and the other, from the thousand or so lead net sinkers that were strewn around, was almost certainly a fishing boat.

A third boat from Blackfriars, which had sunk with a cargo of bricks, was of similar clinker build but has been dated to the seventeenth century.[5] All these craft probably differed little in construction and appearance from the Norman landing ships depicted in the Bayeux Tapestry hundreds of years before. Many early illustrations of the river show similar craft, usually sloop-rigged and obviously good sea-boats for work in rough waters of the estuary when bringing up cargoes of produce from Kent and Essex.

Long before travel by coach and horses was possible, fast sailing tilt boats reminiscent of Viking longships were carrying passengers and light goods between London and Gravesend, a distance of 26

92 A Panoramic View of London (detail), 1749.
Fishing boats lie at anchor and to the left Western barges
cluster alongside Queenhithe dock. Cranes stand over
the waterfront, particularly at the Three Cranes wharf
and stairs on the right. (S. and N. Buck)

miles through waters that could sometimes be hazardous. The Gravesend boats were quite large, carrying a maximum of 37 passengers. Smaller tilt boats went upstream to the west, their square sails augmented by several pairs of oars, many probably carrying members of royal households with their supplies to places such as Richmond Palace, Hampton Court and Windsor Castle. For shorter journeys people hired smaller broad-beamed skiff-like open rowing boats called wherries. The wherrymen waited for fares at their boats on the foreshore like modern drivers waiting in a taxi rank, or touted for customers at the top of the river stairs and along the narrow alleys. In 1603 John Stow in his *Survey of*

London states that at that time there were 3000 watermen working 2000 wherries and small boats, apart from 'Those huge Tideboats, Tilt boats and barges'.

The voyages of Elizabethan and later explorers opened up trade routes to formerly unknown continents, which soon brought ships in their hundreds from all over the world to London River. Through the years ships coming up to London had grown too large to berth at riverside quays and now had to lay at anchor in the Pool of London below the bridge. Therefore London became a lighterage port, all cargoes being transferred between ship and quay by lighters or 'lightening' barges. Early lighters were flat-bottomed, clinker-built boats, only capable of carrying cargoes of barrels and sacks which could be easily manhandled. The later importation of heavy goods such as timber, handled by ships' derricks and quayside cranes, meant that craft of greater capacity were needed and the large box-like swim-headed lighters we know today were developed.

Apart from a swim-headed bow, these later short dumpy lighters had little in common with the long, slim Western barges, which probably evolved much earlier on the upper river. But they were cheap to build and eminently suitable as water-born boxes to convey goods between ship and shore, and as floating warehouses when goods were not needed immediately.

WATERMEN AND LIGHTERMEN

Many estimates have been given over the centuries to try to illustrate the impressive number of people employed on the lower Thames. For instance, during the reign of Elizabeth I the total number of watermen between Windsor and Gravesend was given as 40,000! Obviously there had to be some sort of control over such a large workforce, operating in a sometimes dangerous environment, with many temptations such as extortion from passengers, incompetent boat handling and the theft of goods in transit.

93   A Panoramic View of London (detail), 1749. Wherries ply for hire at Dowgate and Steelyard stairs, a state barge heads towards a peter boat where the crew haul the net. A 'pink' sterned fishing smack with central fish well sails upstream on a stern breeze. (S. and N. Buck)

The first Act of Parliament to control the conduct of wherrymen and bargemen came in 1514. Further acts followed, after continuing complaints of incompetence and disorderly behaviour, and apprenticeships were made compulsory for anyone who wanted to work on the local craft. The Watermen and Lightermen's Company gained considerable powers in 1700, and from that time the Freemen of the Company had a virtual monopoly of working between ship and shore, and plying for hire.

From the fifteenth century many watermen found employment with the ornate ceremonial barges of the nobility, and the city livery companies who competed with each other for the smartest crews, sweetest music and largest banners on the grand river processions on Lord Mayor's Day and other state occasions. The size of these beautiful craft varied considerably, from 45ft (13.5m) shallops to vast 90ft (27m) barges, all clinker-built, with flared, raking bows similar to the wherries. The forward half of the larger vessels had space for about nine pairs of oarsmen, while the stern half held a carved and gilded cabin, often with an upper deck for orchestra or spectators.

By the eighteenth century the watermen and lightermen and their families formed the largest part of a very close-knit riverside community. Sailing ships of many nations now lay in the Pool. (The Upper Pool being from London Bridge to Wapping and the Lower Pool from Wapping to Limehouse, total distance about two miles). Daniel Defoe records that on one occasion he counted no less than 2000 sailing ships lying in the Pool. Fleets of from 500 to 700 collier ships sometimes came up together for their cargo to be discharged at Billingsgate. Three-thousand-five-hundred lighters were in use, carrying cargoes to and from a multitude of wharfs on both sides of the river.

There is no doubt that London could never have evolved as a great port without lighterage. The working of a lighter, more often called a barge or punt, carrying up to 50 tons, was a highly skilled art. It was primarily the ebb and flow of the tide which moved them from place to place for several miles on either side of the Pool. They were usually manned by a single Freeman, who may sometimes have also carried an apprentice, working 'under oars'. Some headway could be achieved with the use of the pair of 30ft (9m) sweeps at the bow, but often a sweep was taken to the stern and used as a steering oar when moving with wind and tide.

94   Billingsgate Wharf, 1859. Essex well-smacks unload at the recently enlarged market, designed in Italian style by J. B. Bunning. The tower held the bell which was traditionally rung to start the daily business at 5 a.m. The market was enlarged again from 1874. (From *The Book of the Thames*)

An intimate knowledge of the river at all states of the tide was vital to achieve a landing at a particular wharf or ship, particularly as the fairway was often cluttered with so many moored and moving craft. In places the tide sets across the river at most peculiar angles, particularly at bends and bridges, and sometimes goes in two different directions at once. Lining up to shoot a particular bridge arch is an art in itself, especially when other craft have the same idea.[6]

THE TIDEWAY FISHERMEN
Until the extermination of life in the tidal Thames by man-made pollution in the nineteenth century, the river supplied an abundance of fish of many species which supported many communities of fishermen all along the upper tideway and on the estuary creeks and rivers. Various nets and traps were employed to catch many different species, but on the shallow upper river the long or seine net was the favourite during the annual salmon runs.

From early times the fishermen of the upper tideway, usually known as petermen, had to con-

form to byelaws laid down by the Lord Mayor's Courts of Conservancy, which restricted their numbers and dictated such things as the mesh size of nets, to prevent the taking of immature stock. Petermen fished the whole of the tidal river down to Leigh, but were not allowed to go further west than Richmond, where they probably came into contact with private freshwater fisheries.

The peterboats which they used had developed like the skiff and wherry from early clinker-built Saxon or Viking craft. They were double-ended, very broad in the beam and very flat on the water, the top strake being perfectly horizontal. There was a boxed-off well in the centre of the boat where the catch could be kept fresh, for at that point there were holes in the bottom and sides of the boat for water

95 The Pool of London, *c.* 1830. An English hay barge and a Dutch coaster drift up with the tide among larger merchant ships. Meanwhile a wherryman carrying supplies inadvertently interrupts the labours of the petermen. (Sir A. W. Callcutt)

circulation. The smaller craft usually had a crew of two, one rowing from the forward end, the other shooting and hauling the net from the stern.

Large sailing peterboats were developed in the nineteenth century for fishing the estuary. Here they competed with hundreds of other small sailing craft from ancient communities on the adjacent coastline and rivers of Kent and Essex, who had fished the rich estuary sandbanks and mudflats for centuries. Their boats were small sailing trawlers, smacks and bawleys, dragging various types of net through shallow waters for flat-fish, whitebait, sprats and mackerel, while others caught shrimps and lobsters or dredged for oysters.

At the end of the nineteenth century hundreds of craft still sailed from the Colne and Medway. On the Thames, Gravesend still had 30 fishing and Leigh 86. Some of the early boats, particularly from Leigh, were clinker-built and double-ended, being called sharp or pink-sterned. Later on, square or counter-sterns and carvel building became the norm.[7]

Once a good catch had been obtained the important thing was to get it to market in good condition, as quickly as possible. That market was normally Billingsgate. To achieve this, most craft had fish wells built into the hull. If catches were light, fish were sometimes kept in specially built coast ponds until there were enough to take up the river. From the beginning of the eighteenth century large well-smacks were built specifically for the carriage of fish upstream to Billingsgate; some catches being sold direct from small fishing boats to the well-smacks while at sea. This trade was continued into the twentieth century by small steam-powered fish carriers, but today the catch from many coasts reaches Billingsgate by road or rail transport, and the five a.m. ritual of unloading from boats moored at the old floating quay is a part of history. Or perhaps not; the pollution has gone and the fish have returned to the river. There are thriving eel fisheries again on the tideway and perhaps soon commercial catches of salmon will once again be landed at a Billingsgate quay.

THE TIDEWAY BARGES

As eighteenth-century London swallowed up the villages and fields around it, the expanding population demanded food and materials from many parts of England. Livestock were driven to market along great drove roads for scores of miles, and farm carts and great lumbering stage wagons daily brought farm and market garden produce to the capital. The river also played a vital role in this trade, with many West Country barges plying the upper tideway. Different types of barges joined them at the London wharfs; the barges of the lower tideway and the Medway, commonly called hoys, bringing up from Kent and Essex fruit and vegetables and building materials of timber, stone, bricks and lime. Some of the most important cargoes were hay and straw, brought in for London's escalating population of carriage and dray horses, and naturally the end product, manure, was also disposed of by the barges, taken back to fertilize the fields which fed London.

The hoys were flat-bottomed, swim-headed sailing craft, similar to large lighters but of massive construction to withstand rough waters, and the wear and tear of lying on shingle and sand at small country wharfs with a heavy load, while waiting for the tide to lift them off. Masts and rigging were much sturdier than those on West Country barges. Some were sloop or cutter-rigged, but most had spritsails – of Dutch origin – the 'sprit' or 'spreet' being a large spar from near the foot of the mast, diagonally up to the peak of the large mainsail, which was otherwise loose-footed.

Pyne's drawings, in his *Microcosm* of 1802, perfectly illustrate the massive construction of these craft. The spritsail rigging was ingeniously arranged to be handled easily by a crew of two. Masts were stepped in a tabernacle, and a large windlass and stayfall tackle at the bow allowed standing sails and rigging to be let down at one go if necessary, especially when negotiating low bridges. The windlass was also needed to weigh anchor. The fore-and-aft sails allowed reasonable performances when beating to windward, but as there was no keel, leeboards, another Dutch introduction, were needed to stop sideways drift.

The accommodation on these barges was usually a small stern cabin, or just a hooped awning like West Country barges, and similar crude tiller steering was employed to control the massive rudder. Barges that carried cargoes such as barrels, timber or straw had open holds, but when perishable or dangerous freight such as gunpowder or lime was carried, water-tight hatch covers were fitted over the enclosed holds.

96 Low tide at Chiswick, *c.* 1890. Barge *Vera*, with hatch covers off, sits comfortably on the hard-packed gravel foreshore

From the mid nineteenth century, possibly due to influences from the River Severn and Kennet and Avon Canal barge builders, major hull improvements were made to spritsail barges. Although the mid-section retained the flat bottom and hard chine for lying aground, bows became much more rounded, and transom sterns replaced the old undercut budgett sterns.

Although small simple 'stumpy' barges with single fore and mainsail continued to be used, particularly for river work, the majority of barges were built for trade through the unpredictable waters of the east coast, and their sailing capabilities were vastly improved with finer hull lines and more sophisticated sails and rigging. Most vessels now had a topsail, extra jib-sails and a bowsprit and a small sprit-rigged mizzen sail. Wheel steering replaced the ordinary tiller, and with the help of several sets of small hand winches, the rigging was so arranged that even the biggest steel barges, carrying up to about 200 tons, could still be handled at most times by just

the skipper and his mate, who was sometimes his wife, or just a boy. Extra help was needed when going 'above bridges' on the Thames or Medway, when a 'huffler' was employed for his local knowledge and help on the windlass, raising and lowering the sailing gear.

Throughout the Victorian era trading areas were extended until the distinctive barges with their rich red/brown sails could be seen at times transferring cargoes at harbours all around Britain and crossing the Irish Sea and English Channel. Several big barges even crossed the Atlantic. Over 2000 barges, with loading capabilities varying from 40 to 120 tons, were in service by 1914, carrying a great variety of goods, including War Department munitions, bricks and cement, fertilizers and city rubbish, and farm produce such as grain and hay.

They served the country well in two World Wars. It was said that barges could go wherever a seagull could swim, and the great skill of their skippers meant that they could take supplies to small tidal creeks or beaches where no other vessel would venture. A number were sunk or badly damaged, and heroic crews were killed by enemy mines and air raids. Thames spritsail barges formed part of the

97 Barge *Alfred* and lighters unloading at Putney, 1878. Fulham church stands on the far bank, above the old wooden Putney bridge and ugly iron aqueduct of the Chelsea Water Works Company

armada of little ships which saved so many men during the evacuation of Dunkirk.

In 1939 there were still 600 barges trading, but the ravages of war and the modern reliance on speedier road and rail transport had reduced their numbers to 180 in 1950. By 1966, although some motor barges were still trading, only *Cambria* was working under sail alone. She is now part of the Maritime Trust collection in the St Katherine Docks. In recent years there has been a great revival of interest in these historic craft, and, in spite of the escalating costs of restoration and upkeep about 80, all at least 50 years old, are now being restored or already sailing as training vessels, barge-yachts, and on promotion or charter work. Several organizations, including the

Thames Sailing Barge Club and the Society for Spritsail Barge Research, are actively engaged in maintaining the sailing skills and undertaking historical research and conservation of these craft.

THE LONDON DOCKS

For centuries the Port of London consisted of legal or state quays which, apart from Queenhithe, were situated between London Bridge and the Tower. Many other sufferance wharfs, on both sides of the river, and run by private companies, usually handled particular goods. Therefore we have Wool Quay, Fish Quay, Timber Hythe, etc. The collection of shipping dues was administered by the officers of the Custom House, conveniently situated next to Billingsgate.

During the late eighteenth century the London riverside was becoming overcrowded with wharfs, warehouses and repair yards, and the Pool itself was at times seriously congested with shipping. Goods

were sometimes left on board ship or lighter for weeks on end, leading to serious losses by spoilage or theft.

The idea of enclosed docks built off the river, with lock gates to hold in the water at one level independent of the ebb and flow of the tide, was not a new one. Henry VIII established a royal dockyard at Woolwich for the building and repair of warships, and in the seventeenth century the East India Company built fitting out docks at Blackwall. However, the first Act for the construction of enclosed docks in London specifically for merchant ships to load and unload was authorized in 1799. The promoters were the City of London and the West India Company. The site chosen utilized an earlier unsuccessful canal which cut across the neck of the area known as the Isle of Dogs, which is enclosed by the great southerly loop of the Thames between Limehouse and Bow Creek.

These docks were opened in 1802. Here at last large ships could lay close to stone quays and cargoes transferred by crane direct from the ships' holds to huge five storey warehouses. To ensure the safety of the vast wealth of goods imported from the West Indies the whole area was sealed off by high walls

98 A 'Stackie', c. 1900, with bowsprit steeved up and an unusual lugsail on the mizzen mast, sails up on the flood, past Paul's Wharf and other great warehouses of the Victorian era

and policed by armed men.

Other great dock systems soon took many ships off the river moorings. The London Docks at Wapping, designed by Rennie, were completed in 1805. The St Katherine Docks, next to the Tower, were opened in 1828. Other docks known to generations of sailors the world over followed; the East India, Millwall, Surrey, the modern 'Royals' and of course Tilbury.

The dredging of shoals to deepen the river for shipping, and to obtain sand and gravel, had been done for centuries. Even so, large ships such as the East Indiamen could never go up into the Pool without fear of going aground at low water. The adaptation of steam engines to drive great floating bucket dredgers meant that at about the same time as the docks were being built, navigable channels of consistent width and depth could now be made from the upper reaches of the tideway to the estuary.

Reaches not far below the Pool, that once had a depth of only one fathom at low water, now have three or more. The charting and marking of the channel out into the estuary with lights and bouys is still undertaken by the ancient establishment of Trinity House.

The building of the enclosed docks did not herald the end of shipping in the Pool. Dredging allowed some large ships to reach some of the riverside wharfs. There was still plenty of work for several more generations of lightermen, taking freight to and from the new docks sytems and riverside warehouses, on to the canal system through Limehouse Basin and up the river to Brentford Dock. The lighter and bargemen were now often assisted by steam tugs, some of which were employed in work-

ing ships in and out of the docks. Strings of lighters could now be taken to their destinations without waiting for the tide to assist them.

The administration of the tidal river was passed from the City of London Corporation to the Thames Conservancy in 1857. Their duties included the regulation of river traffic and maintenance of the dredged channel. In 1909 the Conservancy's area of operations was restricted to the non-tidal river and the new Port of London Authority took over the running of the river from Teddington lock to Yanlet Creek near the mouth of the Medway.

In the mid twentieth century, for reasons much too complicated to discuss here, the Port of London fell into decline. Only the India and Millwall group, part of the Royal Docks, plus the new container and bulk terminals at Tilbury are now operating. The total annual tonnage handled through the port now exceeds 50 million, far less in real terms than before the war, and few ships now enter the Pool to provide work for the thousands that used to rely on them.

99   Shipping on London River, c. 1878. A barque bound for the docks is towed by a twin funnelled paddle tug past a deeply laden spritsail barge

The statistics are astronomical for the variety and quantity of shipping and goods once exported and imported through London to and from practically every country in the world. Exports in 1936 included nearly 1½ million tons of cement, 612,000 tons of iron and steel, 480,000 tons of petroleum and 283,000 tons of cereals. Imports included over 2 million tons of cereals, 3 million tons of timber, 1 million tons of woodpulp, 1 million tons of sugar, 600,000 tons of metals, 600,000 tons of meat, and lesser quantities of gums, hides, skins, tallow, spices, tusks, etc. In 1936 a total of 43 million tons was handled through the port. The number of ships passing in and out totalled 61,132.[8]

These few figures demonstrate how important the river had become to the nation since that day long ago when a few foreign merchants set up shop on the shores of the Thames in the wake of the Roman legions.

With the end of large-scale commerce on London River, much of old dockland has been swept away. Fortunately some of the large and imposing Victorian warehouse facades have been preserved for posterity – some as small offices, some converted to homes. To some people they symbolize our greatness as a trading nation, while to others they may represent a long history of oppression and the forceful acquisition of animal and mineral resources from overseas.

In recent years Londoners were becoming increasingly aware that the river which was once their lifeline might one day swamp them. These fears were allayed with the completion of the Thames Barrier across the Woolwich Reach. It will protect them from the sea for decades to come. Hopefully its eventual replacement will be a system of locks and weirs below London, to turn the Thames into a clear, freshwater tideless river all the way from Teddington. Schemes such as this have been seriously discussed from at least the beginning of this century. If the idea is ever implemented, the river could once more become a thriving waterway, perhaps not for the carriage of merchandise, but as twenty miles or more of wide, safe river for mainly recreational use, providing work for countless small businesses on its banks. This would be a focus for a multitude of activities, from fish farming to tourism and waterborne sports of all kinds. It could then be as busy with pleasure boats as the middle Thames is today, and as this highway of London itself was centuries ago.

100   Tower Bridge, c. 1900. The bascules are raised for a coaster going up on the tide. Lighters cluster by Butler's Wharf, while two of vastly differing size are under oars

Notes

CHAPTER 1

1. S. McGrail, *Logboats of England and Wales*, National Maritime Museum, Series 2 – B.A.R. British Series, 51, 1978.

2. F. S. Thacker, *Thames Highway, Vol. 1 General History*, Thacker, 1914.

3. H. M. Colvin, ed., *History of the Kings Works, Vol. 1*, HMSO, 1963.

4. E. Stone, ed., *The Oxfordshire Hundred Rolls of 1279*, Oxfordshire Record Society, 1968.

5. Colvin, op. cit.

6. Singer, Holmyard, etc., eds., *A History of Technology*, Clarendon Press, 1957.

7. P.R.O. KB 26/150.

CHAPTER 2

1. Tighe and Davis, *Annals of Windsor*, Longman, Brown, 1858.

2. P.R.O. Pipe Roll no. 183 (12 Edward III) M.47.

3. Abingdon Abbey Treasurers Accounts 1383–4, Abingdon Corporation. Translation in W. O. Hassall, *They saw it happen, 55 BC–AD 1485*, Blackwell.

4. C. Hohler, 'Medieval Paving Tiles in Bucks', *Records of Bucks XIV*.

5. *Lord Boston's Notes*, Buckinghamshire Arch. Soc.

6. 'Household Accounts of Windsor Castle', Tighe and Davis, op. cit.

7. C. L. Kingsford, ed., *The Stonor Letters and Papers*, Camden III Series, Royal Historical Society, 1919.

8. S. T. Bindoff, 'Clement Armstrong and his treatises of the Commonwealth', *Economic History Review, Vol. 14*, 1944–5.

9. Dr M. Prior, *Fisher Row*, Clarendon Press, 1982.

10. Dr M. Prior, 'The Accounts of Thomas West of Wallingford', *Oxononiensia*, Vol. 46, 1981.

CHAPTER 3

1. P. Marsden, 'Celtic Ships of Europe', *Sources and Techniques in Boat Archaeology*, B.A.R., Supplementary Series, 29, 1977.

2. M. D. de Weerd, 'Ships of the Roman period at Zwammerdam' in Taylor and Cleere, eds., *Roman shipping and trade*, C.B.A. Research Report No. 24, 1978.

3. P. Marsden, *A Roman Ship from Blackfriars, London*, Guildhall Museum, 1966.

4. Chew and Kellaway, eds., *The London Assize of Nuisance*, 1301–1431, London Record Society, 1973.

5. A. Wood, *City of Oxford, Vol. 1.*, ed. A. Clark, Clarendon Press, 1889.

6. F. G. G. Carr, *Sailing Barges*, Peter Davies, 1951.

CHAPTER 4

1. T. Gillmer, 'The Capability of the single square sail rig', in S. McGrail, ed., *Medieval Ships and Harbours in Northern Europe*, National Maritime Museum Series No. 5, B.A.R. International Series 66, 1979.

2. Wye Barge Exhibition, Monmouth Museum, 1978.

3. *Buckinghamshire Quarter Sessions Records*, Bucks County Record Office.

4. Kenton Theatre, Henley.

CHAPTER 5

1. P.R.O *Proceedings in Star Chamber*, STAC 8 164/9.

2. Based on a sketch map probably drawn by Rowland Hynde, Lord of the Manor of Hedsor, during a dispute with his neighbour, Henry Manfield of Cliveden. Notes on the original read:

1. The Warboro.
This part of the Warboro pulled up by Manfield since the council commanded the contrary.

2. Manfield felled since Christmas last one hundred trees upon Sashes whereby he might draw up by barge by Hyndes water which with his horses he did attempt to do two times in March last, but did not prevail, as by affidavit appeareth.

3. The antient channel of Theames doth now run wholly within ye County of Buckinghamshire and if Manfield tourne it through Sashes Water it will then run altogether within ye County of Barkshire.

2. J. Carter and J. Smith, *Give and Take, History of Christ's Hospital, Abingdon 1553–1900*, Carter and Smith, 1981.

4. A. W. Skempton, 'Canals and River Navigations before 1750', in Singer, Holmyard, eds., *A History of Technology Vol. III*, Clarendon Press, 1957.

5. J. Taylor, 'Carriers Cosmographie', in Arber, *English Garner, Vol. I.*

6. A. Carter and J. Stevenson, *The Oxfordshire area in the Civil War*, B.B.C. Radio Oxford Publications.

7. Tighe and Davis, op. cit.

8. Bucks Quarter Sessions Records, quoted in Wilson, *The Making of the Middle Thames.*

CHAPTER 7

1. G. Farr, 'Severn Navigation and the Trow', in *Mariners Mirror, Vol. 32*, 1940.

2. H. Household, *The Thames and Severn Canal*, David and Charles, 1969.

3. W. Mavor, *General View of the Agriculture of Berkshire*, 1809.

4. F. S. Thacker, *Kennet Country*, Blackwell, 1932.

CHAPTER 8

1. The Byelaws of The Thames Commissioners, 1804. Thames Water Archives, Reading.

2. G. Farr, op. cit.

3. R. B. Wilson, ed., *Sir Daniel Gooch, Memoirs and Diary*, David and Charles, 1972.

4. Thames Water Archives, Reading.

CHAPTER 9

1. F. S. Thacker, *Kennet Country*, Blackwell, 1932.

2. John Gould, Pers. Comm.

3. Canal Notes, Cirencester Library.

4. David Wood, '*Hope* from above Guildford', *Topsail, Journal of the Society for Spritsail Barge Research*, No. 17, 1978.

5. Guildford Muniment Room, Surrey Record Office.

6. M. Denney, *London and South East England, Historic Waterways Scenes*, Morland, 1980.

7. Thames Water, *Instructions to lockstaff book*, c. 1926.

8. Report of Thames Conservancy Board Meeting, January 1928.

CHAPTER 10

1. B. Hobley, 'The London Waterfront', in G. Milne and B. Hobley, eds., *Waterfront Archaeology in Britain and N. Europe*, C.B.A. Research Report No. 41, 1981.

2. P. Marsden, *A Roman ship from Blackfriars, London*, Guildhall Museum, 1966.

3. A. Schofield, 'Medieval Waterfront buildings' in Milne and Hobley, op. cit.

4. 'An Antiquary', *Chronicles of London Bridge*, Thomas Tegg, London, 1839.

5. P. Marsden, 'The Medieval Ships of London' in S. McGrail, *Medieval ships and Harbours in N. Europe*, National Maritime Museum, Arch. ser. 5., B.A.R. International ser. 66, 1979.

6. H. Harris, *Under Oars, Reiminiscences of a Thames Lighterman 1894–1909*, Centerprise Trust Ltd., and Stepney Books Publications, 1978.

7. E.J. March, *Inshore Craft of Britain, Vol. 1*, David and Charles, 1970.

8. A. Bell, *The Said Noble River*, Port of London Authority, 1937.

Bibliography

THAMES BOOKS WITH ILLUSTRATIONS
ON NAVIGATION WORKS AND CRAFT

ARMSTRONG, W., *The Thames from its rise to the Nore*, Virtue, 1886.

BROWN, B., ed. *The England of Henry Taunt*, Routledge and Kegan Paul, 1973.

BYRNE, L. S. R., and CHURCHILL, E. L., *The Eton book of the river*. Spottiswoode and Ballantyne, 1935.

CARR, F. G. G., *Sailing barges*, Peter Davies, 1951.

COMBE, W., *An History of the River Thames* (Farington prints), Boydell, 1793/4.

COOKE, W. B., and COOKE, G., *Views on the Thames*, 1822.

COOKE, W. B., and OWEN, S., *The Thames*, 1811.

FEARNSIDE, W. G., *Thames and Medway* (80 engravings by Tombleson), Black and Armstrong, 1834).

HALL, MR and MRS S. C., *The Book of the Thames*, Virtue, 1859.

HAVELL, W., *Picturesque views of the River Thames*, 1812.

HERBERT, A. P., *The Thames*, Weidenfeld and Nicholson, 1966.

IRELAND, S., *Picturesque views on the River Thames*, 1791.

JONES, S. R., *Thames Triumphant*, The Studio Publications, 1943.

LEYLAND, J., *The Thames Illustrated*, G. Newnes, c. 1900.

LINNEY, A. G., *Lure and lore of London's river*, Sampson Low and Marston, 1931.

PHILLIPS, H., *The Thames about 1750*, Collins, 1951.

ROBERTSON, H. R., *Life on the upper Thames*, Virtue and Spalding, 1875.

ROLT, L. T. C., *The Thames from Mouth to Source*, Batsford, 1951.

TAUNT, H., *Illustrated Map of the Thames*, Oxford c. 1880.

THACKER, F., *Thames Highway, Vol. 1., General History*, London, 1914.

THACKER, F., *Thames Highway, Vol. 2., Locks and Weirs*, London, 1920.

Thames Conservancy Centenary Handbook, 1957.

THORNE, J., *Rambles by Rivers, The Thames*, 1847.

WESTHALL, W., and OWEN, S., *Picturesque tour of the River Thames*, 1828.

WILSON, D. G., *The Making of the Middle Thames*, Spurbooks, 1977.

Index